Copyright © 2025 by Luke Hall

Published by Four Rivers Media

All rights reserved. No portion of this book may be reproduced, stored in a retrieval system, or transmitted in any form or by any means—electronic, mechanical, photocopy, recording, scanning, or other—except for brief quotations in critical reviews or articles, without prior written permission of the author.

Unless otherwise specified, all Scripture quotations are taken from the Holy Bible, New International Version®, NIV®. Copyright © 1973, 1978, 1984, 2011 by Biblica, Inc.™ Used by permission of Zondervan. All rights reserved worldwide. www.zondervan.com. The "NIV" and "New International Version" are trademarks registered in the United States Patent and Trademark Office by Biblica, Inc.™ | Scripture quotations marked ESV are from The ESV® Bible (The Holy Bible, English Standard Version®), copyright © 2001 by Crossway, a publishing ministry of Good News Publishers. Used by permission. All rights reserved. | Scripture quotations marked KJV are taken from the King James Version of the Bible. Public domain. | Scripture quotations marked NKJV are taken from the New King James Version®. Copyright © 1982 by Thomas Nelson. Used by permission. All rights reserved.

For foreign and subsidiary rights, contact the author.

Cover design by Sara Young

ISBN: 978-1-964794-55-6   1 2 3 4 5 6 7 8 9 10

Printed in the United States of America

THE LEAD MODEL

*Understanding How You Lead
and Who You Lead*

DR. LUKE S. HALL

CONTENTS

Introduction 11

CHAPTER 1. **Every Leader Needs Self-Assessment**.... 15
CHAPTER 2. **Connected but Not Compatible** 29
CHAPTER 3. **The Fearless Leader:** *A Lion's Roar* 49
CHAPTER 4. **The Visionary Leader:**
　　　　　　An Eagle's-Eye Vision 67
CHAPTER 5. **The Unseen Leader:** *An Ant's Mission*....... 93
CHAPTER 6. **The Peaceful Leader:**
　　　　　　A Dove's Quiet Power 105
CHAPTER 7. **Four Personalities, One Vision:** *Unlocking the
　　　　　　Synergy of the LEAD Model Team* 119
Group Discussion Questions 137
Leadership Activity 141

INTRODUCTION

12 THE **LEAD** MODEL

WHILE SITTING IN AN EMPTY parking lot contemplating whether I had the mental bandwidth to continue serving as pastor, I looked into the rearview mirror of my vehicle and asked myself, "Who preaches to the preacher?"

In my search for answers, I stumbled upon a study. As of March 2022, 42 percent of pastors reported having considered quitting full-time ministry.[1] By late 2023, that figure had risen to 53 percent.[2]

Many attribute this staggering number to stress, depression, isolation, or simple burnout. Many pastors feel as if they have no one to help carry the weight of ministry. I believe that this percentage could be eliminated or at least drastically decreased if they only had help—not just any help but the right help.

---

1 Barna, "Pastors Share Top Reasons They've Considered Quitting Ministry in the Past Year," *Barna*, 27 Apr. 2022, https://www.barna.com/research/pastors-quitting-ministry/?utm_source=chatgpt.com.
2 Leonardo Blair, "With rising discontent, more than half of American clergy seriously considered quitting: study," *The Christian Post*, 11 Jan. 2024, https://www.christianpost.com/news/over-half-of-american-pastors-have-considered-quitting-poll.html?utm_source=chatgpt.com.

While serving as the executive pastor of a flourishing ministry, I was often called upon to mediate disputes or disagreements among the leaders and those serving with them in ministry. These monthly or sometimes weekly calls were very taxing and draining, but I was determined to protect the senior pastor from these issues so that he could be free to focus on moving the church forward, hearing from God, and preparing for his weekly sermons.

So, I simply addressed the issues the best I could, even if that meant replacing leaders, adding more volunteers, taking the ministry leaders out to lunch, giving them gift cards, greeting cards, or letters of appreciation, and even an occasional one-on-one counseling session.

I would prop the ministries up the best I could so that they would appear fertile and flourishing, but I soon discovered that problems and dysfunction cannot be covered up forever. In other words: "Imitations have limitations; the truth will be revealed." I discovered that whatever you allow as a leader, you, in essence, condone.

The truth is that I was selecting ministry leaders who didn't quite fit their roles. I was adding willing volunteers who weren't necessarily able volunteers for that ministry. Unfriendly and uninviting greeters affected the church members' attitudes before they were even seated. I found out through trial and error that a willing person is not always an able person.

The Bible emphasizes the importance of placing the right people in the right roles, particularly in leadership and service.

Moses's father-in-law, Jethro, observed that Moses sat all alone to judge the people from morning until evening. Jethro noticed the long lines, the needy people—he saw from a distance all the things that Moses was doing to serve the people with no help. Jethro immediately said to Moses, "This is not good for you! You can't be all things to all people; you need help!" He advised Moses to appoint leaders who were capable, God-fearing, trustworthy, and honest to help govern the people (Exodus 18:14-21).

This book is written to help pastors like Moses—and like me—discover, develop, and deploy the right kind of help for their mission.

CHAPTER 1

EVERY LEADER NEEDS SELF-ASSESSMENT

WHEN BUILDING A TEAM, IT is vitally important that leaders understand self-assessment—the foundation of leadership selection. The success or failure of a leadership team is often set in motion long before the first decision is made and the first challenge is faced. It begins the moment the first team member is selected. William Shakespeare, in his play *Hamlet*, said it best: "To thine own self be true."[3] But how can a pastor or ministry leader choose the right people without first understanding themselves? Before evaluating potential team members, pastors and other first-level leaders must first take a deep, intrinsic look at themselves and evaluate their own strengths, weaknesses, developmental challenges, and leadership traits.

Every leader embodies a unique combination of leadership traits. Some leaders have a natural dominance, pushing forward with bold vision, while others lead with clarity and can see the

---

3 William Shakespeare, *Hamlet,* ed. Barbara A. Mowat and Paul Werstine (New York, NY: Washington Square Press, 1992), 1.3.78.

big picture, though they often miss the fine details. Some leaders operate with relentless diligence, ensuring every process runs smoothly, while others bring a gentle and relational spirit to the team that fosters unity and care. All of these traits are important and add value to a team, but it is the first-level leader's responsibility to position each team member according to these traits so that they can all work together in unison.

Leaders who choose to ignore this vital step of self-awareness may unknowingly gravitate toward individuals who mirror their own personal strengths, resulting in a team with blind spots and undiagnosed weaknesses. By first assessing oneself honestly, a leader can approach team selection with wisdom and safeguard against building a team that's unbalanced, ineffective, and more competitive than complementary.

In this chapter, we will explore the critical role that self-assessment plays in leadership selection and how unchecked biases and blind spots can lead to dysfunction, stagnation, and, ultimately, the demise of the team. It's been said that things don't end wrong; they begin wrong. So, hopefully, you will use the practical steps in this book to align your team with both your vision and mission. Selecting the right team isn't just about choosing strong team members; it's about choosing team members who strengthen the leader, complement the team, and successfully accomplish the mission—and that begins with self-assessment.

James's words offer a powerful metaphor for leadership—what it means to be "the leader in the mirror":

Anyone who listens to the word but does not do what it says is like someone who looks at his face in a mirror and, after looking at himself, goes away and immediately forgets what he looks like.
—James 1:23-24

James's analogy of a mirror invites us into a transformative process, which is the act of self-assessment. Just as a mirror reflects an image, self-assessment reveals the truths about our identity, strengths, weaknesses, and spiritual health. However, the challenge lies in what we do with that reflection. Do we examine it deeply and make changes accordingly, or do we turn away, forgetting what we've seen, only to have to deal with the consequences of a broken team, ministry, or even church?

SELF-ASSESSMENT IS NOT INTROSPECTION

A spiritual self-assessment goes beyond surface-level introspection. Self-assessment is the intentional process of looking inward to evaluate aspects of your identity that define your self-esteem, self-worth, and self-value. This reflective process can either build you up or tear you down, depending on how honestly and graciously you engage with it. A deep stare into the mirror of life will reveal whether you are making progress or remaining more stagnant than you had expected. Remember, movement is not always progress, and consistency is not always indicative of growth.

At its core, self-assessment forces you to confront the parts of yourself that are easy to ignore or hide from others. It is a courageous act to examine the side of you that you don't want anyone else to see. Yet, this vulnerability is necessary for spiritual growth, deeper relationships, and a clearer sense of purpose.

It is designed to:

- **Clarify spiritual identity:** Understanding who you are in Christ and your role in His kingdom.
- **Strengthen relationships**: By knowing yourself better, you can relate to others more deeply and foster harmony in your relationships.
- **Support spiritual growth**: Identifying areas of spiritual strength and weakness allows you to focus on growth opportunities and deepen your relationship with God.

When we assess ourselves spiritually, we gain insights into how our thoughts, actions, and attitudes align with God's Word. This process helps us to better understand our fellow laborers in ministry and improves our ability to communicate and serve harmoniously with them.

Self-assessment can easily be misdiagnosed as introspection. Although they both require an internal analysis, their objectives are very different. Introspection involves self-reflection and self-awareness, which allows you to understand your motivations, beliefs, and behaviors. It is the process of examining your own thoughts, emotions, and experiences. This practice fosters deeper insight into your inner self to help with personal growth, emotional regulation, and decision-making.

Introspection and self-assessment are both valuable tools for personal and leadership growth, but in the context of this model, introspection is an inferior process to self-assessment when it comes to running an effective ministry. The key distinctions lie in objectivity, actionability, and alignment with leadership effectiveness. While introspection has its place in personal spiritual growth, it lacks the clarity, structure, and external validation needed for effective ministry leadership. Self-assessment, on the other hand, ensures that leaders are not just feeling their way through leadership but actively measuring and improving their effectiveness.

It is important that leaders not only know themselves but also evaluate themselves against the tangible characteristics that we will discuss in the coming chapters. True leadership requires assessment, refinement, and intentional growth, not just reflection.

Life itself is a mirror that reveals the truth about where you stand. The reflection might show that you are well on your way toward fulfilling your calling, or it might reveal that you've stagnated or veered off course. The question is, will you acknowledge what you see and take steps to grow, or will you turn away and remain unchanged?

During my first year as senior pastor, I had a member whose mother was very ill. The doctors didn't think that she would make it through the night. The member asked if I would come to the hospital to pray for her mother, but I was unavailable, so I sent a senior minister to go on my behalf. The member called me a week later to express how disappointed she was with the visit of the senior minister. Although she was grateful that someone from her church came to pray for her mother, she felt that neither his words nor his prayers were consoling or empathetic. I immediately went to her home, offered my condolences, prayed with her, and convinced her that she should continue attending our church. For many weeks, I avoided addressing the matter with the senior minister because the problem was not solely with his delivery; the problem was with his assignment. If I had only conducted an honest assessment of the senior minister, I would have realized that his natural disposition was not conducive to the assignment. Not only had I not assessed the senior minister, but I had not assessed myself.

> *I sent a person, but she needed the right person.*

Why did I send someone on an assignment based on title alone? Maybe because that's what needed to happen. I was unavailable, so I sent a willing person. However, as the senior pastor, I still had a responsibility. It never crossed my mind that the person I sent could not offer the kind of help that the member needed. I sent *a* person, but she needed *the right* person. Conducting the proper self-assessment on the front end could have saved all parties from this great embarrassment.

BARRIERS TO HONEST SELF-ASSESSMENT

Self-assessment is an essential tool for personal and spiritual growth, yet it is often hindered by internal and external barriers. The ability to honestly reflect on one's strengths and weaknesses can foster maturity and wisdom, not only for individual development but also in evaluating others, especially within leadership contexts. In accordance with the LEAD Model, assessing team members effectively is just as important as self-reflection, as it ensures that the right individuals are placed in roles that align with their strengths. However, fear of vulnerability, pride, comparison, and avoidance can cloud both self-perception and the ability to objectively assess others. Overcoming these obstacles is not usually organic; it requires intentionality, humility, and a willingness to confront uncomfortable truths about yourself and your team members. By understanding these barriers, pastors and other key leaders can cultivate a more authentic and transformative self-assessment model, leading to stronger, more effective teams. Here are a few of the barriers to open and honest self-assessment that I have witnessed during my leadership journey.

Pride and Comparison

It's uncomfortable to confront the parts of yourself that fall short of who you aspire to be. No leader will ever conquer what they are afraid to confront. The fear of vulnerability has the power to keep a leader stuck in a place of disappointment, causing them to become micromanagers, afraid to totally delegate responsibilities out of fear that their limitations may be exposed. Many pastors are afraid to admit what they do not know; they are afraid of hiring people with a skill set that they don't possess, and they are very uncomfortable managing people who may be more knowledgeable than they are in certain areas. This creates a guarded culture with limited trust, collaboration, and transparency. Team members don't feel comfortable demonstrating their gifts and talents, so they muzzle their creativity and do only what's asked of them. Unfortunately, many pastors have been hurt so badly during their journey that they are willing to let their church die so that their image can live. That struggle between self-preservation and selfless leadership is a deep leadership challenge. When a pastor prioritizes their own image and reputation or hides their emotional wounds over the well-being of the church, their ability to discern where team members truly belong will be impaired. A church cannot thrive if the leader is consumed with self-image over self-improvement. True leadership demands humility, discernment, and a willingness to put the mission above personal fears.

Thinking you are on a "different level" than someone else can lead to arrogance and hinder genuine self-examination. This is a dangerous leadership mindset because arrogance creates blind spots in leadership. This leads to misplaced leadership assignments, as roles are filled based on bias or assumptions rather than actual strengths and abilities. When you believe that others are not on your level, it changes the way you treat and interact with them. You may unconsciously distance yourself or judge them unfairly, creating division rather than unity. Some pastors actually wear titles that they have not earned but have given themselves—bishop, apostle, doctor, etc.—all so that they can feel justified in the eyes of their peers. But when pastors assume titles they have not earned, they often do so to gain validation and status rather than to fulfill a true calling. This creates a false sense of authority that distorts their leadership approach, leading to poor team placements within the ministry. Instead of evaluating team members based on gifting, skill, and calling, these leaders may make decisions driven by insecurity, image preservation, or hierarchy reinforcement rather than strategic leadership moves to better the team or ministry.

This mindset causes several leadership dysfunctions. First, it discourages capable leaders from stepping into roles where they can thrive because the pastor may feel threatened by those with true anointing and experience. Second, it creates a culture where titles matter more than effectiveness, meaning unqualified individuals may be placed in key leadership roles simply because they fit the leader's preferred image rather than God's design. Lastly, it fosters a disconnect between leadership and the congregation, as people may sense that appointments are based on status-seeking rather than spiritual discernment.

Avoidance

Ignoring your shortcomings prevents growth and fosters complacency. Avoiding the problem doesn't change the problem; it actually serves as fertilizer that causes the problem to grow.

When a leader ignores their shortcomings, they create an environment of stagnation where neither they nor their team can grow. Avoiding weaknesses doesn't make them disappear; instead, it amplifies dysfunction and promotes poor leadership decisions, including frequent and damaging team misplacement. A leader unwilling to confront their own blind spots will struggle to objectively evaluate the strengths and weaknesses of their team members. This results in filling roles based on convenience, favoritism, or avoidance—rather than true gifting and calling.

By assessing team members and embracing honest self-assessment, pastors can break down these barriers and cultivate an environment of trust, humility, and growth.

Self-assessment enhances understanding of personal and spiritual strengths of team members, which allows for more effective leadership placement, ensuring that each person serves in a role that aligns with their God-given abilities. The LEAD Model emphasizes that when individuals and teams operate in their rightful positions, they not only thrive personally but also thrive as productive members of their teams, ministries, and churches.

STEPS TO CONDUCTING A SPIRITUAL SELF-ASSESSMENT

1) **Pray for guidance**: Begin by asking God for clarity and humility as you reflect on your life.
2) **Examine your reflection**: Ask yourself questions:
   - Am I living in alignment with God's Word?
   - How do my actions reflect my faith?
   - What attitudes or habits do I need to change?
3) **Seek feedback**: Invite trusted mentors or spiritual leaders to provide honest feedback about areas where you can grow.
4) **Repent and adjust**: Acknowledge areas where you fall short and take actionable steps to improve.
5) **Celebrate growth**: Recognize and give thanks for the ways you have grown spiritually and relationally.

A CALL TO ACTION

Take a moment to look into the mirror of life and reflect on your spiritual journey. Are you growing closer to God? Are your relationships thriving? Are you living authentically, or are you hiding behind a facade? The process of self-assessment may be challenging, but it is essential for becoming the person God has called you to be.

> *As leaders, we must be what we want others to become.*

Let James's words guide you: don't walk away from the mirror and forget what you see. Instead, use that reflection as a starting point for transformation, trusting that God will walk with you every step of the way.

Most volunteers are God-fearing, trustworthy, and honest, but not all are capable or have the temperament for all ministries.

As leaders, we must be what we want others to become, and I have discovered that ministries thrive when strong, wise, and compassionate leaders appoint team members who are not just capable but called, not just skilled but spiritually attuned.

Yet, selecting the right people to lead can often feel like an overwhelming challenge.

How do we discern who is truly capable of leadership in ministry?

This book was born out of my deep desire to help pastors and church leaders identify and develop the right individuals for their ministerial teams using four powerful biblical metaphors that characterize the nature of various leaders today: the Lion, the Eagle, the Ant, and the Dove.

As you read this book, I hope that you will allow the LEAD Model to provide a clear and practical framework for recognizing leadership qualities that align with the vision and mission of your ministry. I believe that each of these leadership styles represents distinct characteristics essential to a healthy, thriving, and successful ministry.

As you journey through this book, I invite you to reflect on the different leaders within your ministry, understanding that leadership is not a one-size-fits-all calling but a divine orchestration of different gifts working in harmony to accomplish a unified goal.

My prayer is that this book equips you with the wisdom to choose and cultivate leaders who will strengthen your ministry and lighten your burden. May this LEAD Model serve as both a guide and an inspiration as you seek to lead with discernment, faith, and love.

CHAPTER 2

CONNECTED BUT NOT COMPATIBLE

BUILDING LIFELONG RELATIONSHIPS

I**N 2009, I LAUNCHED NEW** Vision Christian Church from the living room of my home, fueled by faith and a vision for ministry. To help build this foundation, I carefully selected nine people who consisted of friends, co-workers, and relatives, all individuals I trusted and believed in. They all worked well with me in the past on different projects, but I soon realized that working well with me did not mean working well with each other. Though my selections connected them, their temperaments were incompatible. The result was friction, misalignment, and leadership challenges that I had not anticipated. One of the members came to me after a meeting and said, "Luke, I like you, and I am willing to work with you, but I refuse to work with them." This occasion almost ended with a grand opening and a grand closing on the same day. That experience sparked a deeper understanding of what it truly takes to form an effective ministry team—not just assembling people but selecting the right people. I soon realized that everyone I had selected was headstrong, highly opinionated, and very territorial in their point of view. How do I get them to work together on a common goal? Their resumes clearly showed that each of them was highly qualified, but how do you measure temperament? Little did I know that this would be the birthplace not only of the church but of the LEAD Model.

THE DANGER OF MISMATCHED PARTNERSHIPS

> *"Do not be yoked together with unbelievers. For what do righteousness and wickedness have in common? Or what fellowship can light have with darkness?" (2 Corinthians 6:14)*

A yoke is a wooden bar that joins two oxen together, enabling them to pull a load as a team. For the yoke to function effectively, the two oxen must be of similar strength, height, and temperament. If one is stronger or taller than the other, the weaker or shorter ox will slow the team down, causing them to move in circles rather than progress forward.

In the same way, being unequally yoked in relationships, whether in marriage, friendship, or ministry, can create imbalance and conflict. Instead of working together toward a common goal, the individuals find themselves at odds, unable to accomplish what God has called them to do.

Paul's teaching on being "unequally yoked" is often understood as a warning against relationships between believers and unbelievers. However, there's a deeper layer to this principle. Even if both individuals are saved, they can still be unequally yoked if their values, priorities, or goals are misaligned. This dynamic can prevent them from walking in unity and fulfilling their God-given purpose together.

For example, most pastors insist that newly engaged couples complete mandatory premarital counseling before agreeing to officiate a wedding. I require completion of premarital counseling sessions before a wedding date is set. This allows the couple to ask deep, probing questions of each other, absent the pressure of the pre-planned wedding date. Pastors can utilize the LEAD Model to help with this process.

Leadership selection, much like premarital counseling, is not just about finding the right person for the moment but finding the right partner for the mission. It's about understanding compatibility, strengths, and challenges before agreeing to move forward as a team.

In the following sections, I will use the LEAD Model as a foundation and draw parallels between marriage and leadership to demonstrate how different relational dynamics reflect the leadership styles of the Lion, Eagle, Ant, and Dove. Just as a strong marriage requires a balance of personalities and strengths, an effective leadership team must incorporate these diverse traits to ensure that each member is positioned where they can thrive. By exploring how these leadership styles manifest in marital relationships, we gain a deeper understanding of how to identify and place the right individuals in ministry leadership roles.

THE LION: LEADERSHIP AND VISION

In the LEAD Model, the Lion represents boldness, authority, and decisiveness. The Lion is a natural leader—dominant, assertive, and unafraid to make tough decisions. They thrive in taking charge, setting direction, and expecting others to follow through with strength and confidence. While these traits are essential for leadership, they can also lead to stubbornness, control, and unwillingness to compromise when not balanced with other relational styles.

Now, imagine a marriage where both spouses are Lions. On the one hand, this can create a power couple, a dynamic, driven relationship where both partners are strong-willed, goal-oriented, and fearless in making decisions together. They are likely to build a vision for their family, take on challenges head-on, and refuse to back down when facing adversity. However, the same strengths that make them powerful can also become sources of intense conflict. With two dominant personalities, disagreements can escalate into battles for control, as neither wants to back down or appear weak. Decision-making can become a war zone, where both spouses push their agendas, leading to a marriage full of competition rather than collaboration.

In ministry leadership, this same Lion vs. Lion dynamic can lead to conflicting visions, leadership clashes, and an inability to delegate or compromise. Just as a successful Lion marriage requires humility, compromise, and recognizing each other's strengths, a successful leadership team with many Lions does not constantly clash but instead respects one another's leadership while allowing space for the Eagle's vision, the Ant's diligence, and the Dove's peacekeeping influence. A Lion-led ministry team, like a Lion-Lion marriage, will only thrive when each partner learns to lead together rather than against one another.

Like a strong marriage, strong leadership requires vision. Premarital counseling helps couples assess whether they share a unified vision for their future. Just as a man and woman must examine whether they are prepared to lead and serve each other, leaders must also evaluate their ability to guide a team.

The LEAD model serves as an excellent blueprint for understanding couples' leadership styles and how those styles are applied within their marriage. Here's what using the LEAD Model looks like in premarital counseling sessions: if one person in a couple is more of a Lion and the other leans toward the Dove (peacekeeper), Eagle (visionary), or Ant (worker), the couple must learn to balance decision-making and support for a harmonious marriage. A pastor should utilize the model in the same way when selecting a leadership team in ministry. Just as a husband and wife must assess their leadership compatibility, pastors must evaluate the leadership composition of their teams. A team filled with Lions alone can lead to power struggles, while a team without any Lions may lack clear authority and decisive leadership. Having more than one lion on a team can be effective, but success depends on their ability to respect, value, and collaborate with one another. A Lion's bold decision-making works best when it is supported by the visionary insight of the Eagle, the diligence of the Ant, and the relational wisdom of the Dove. If a pastor only surrounds themselves with other Lions, they may experience constant conflict and competition, whereas if they fail to appoint any Lions, the ministry may lack strong leadership and direction. Whether in ministry or marriage, understanding leadership styles is essential to building a partnership that is both effective and harmonious.

THE EAGLE: PERSPECTIVE AND WISDOM

Just as a successful marriage demands the ability to anticipate and navigate future challenges with wisdom, wise leadership requires foresight and adaptability. In marriage, self-assessment in this area ensures that both partners have a realistic view of their strengths and areas for growth before saying, "I do."

In premarital counseling, discovering a couple's relational style and how they envision their future together can serve as an insightful backdrop for the Eagle of the LEAD Model. The Eagle represents vision, foresight, and the ability to see the bigger picture, making it a crucial leadership trait in both marriage and ministry. In a relationship, if one or both partners possess strong Eagle tendencies, they will likely be future-focused, goal-driven, and passionate about pursuing a shared vision. However, challenges may arise if both individuals are so focused on long-term goals that they neglect present relational needs or if one partner has trouble aligning with their partner's vision. A marriage with one Eagle and the other an Ant or a Dove (a more grounded leadership style) requires intentional communication and alignment to ensure that the dreamer does not leave their Ant or Dove feeling unheard or left behind.

This same principle can be applied to leadership team selection in ministry. Just as a couple must navigate their vision for marriage, a pastor must evaluate the presence of Eagles on their leadership team to ensure there is someone who can cast vision, anticipate challenges, and provide direction. However, an Eagle without balance can lead a team that is constantly focused on future goals without ensuring that the authoritative leadership (Lion), foundational work (Ant), and relational dynamics (Dove) are in place. Similarly, just as in marriage, multiple Eagles on the same team without a shared vision can create conflicting directions rather than unified progress. Whether in a marriage or ministry, the Eagle must learn to collaborate, communicate, and recognize the value of other leadership styles to build a strong, sustainable foundation for success.

THE ANT: WORK ETHIC AND COMMITMENT

A strong marriage requires diligence, just as effective leadership demands discipline and commitment. The Ant represents hard work and preparation, both essential for a thriving relationship. Premarital counseling acts as a structured form of self-assessment, allowing couples to evaluate their work ethic in maintaining a relationship. Couples in premarital counseling should be able to answer the question, "Are you willing to put in the effort to build trust, maintain understanding, and resolve conflict?" This question also applies to the leadership selection process.

In premarital counseling, the Ant of the LEAD Model provides a valuable framework for understanding how a couple will approach the work and structure of their marriage. As couples must work like ants, building diligently over time and assessing their readiness to work together in building a strong foundation for their future, they must evaluate their ability to collaborate, stay committed, and handle the daily responsibilities that sustain their relationship. An Ant-driven couple will be hardworking, detail-oriented, and disciplined, ensuring that they are laying bricks for their future rather than just dreaming about it. However, if one partner is highly industrious (Ant) while the other is more of a visionary (Eagle) or authority figure (Lion), conflicts may arise when the Ant feels overburdened with the day-to-day tasks while the other focuses on big-picture goals.

In the same way, a leader must recognize that without the Ants, those who labor behind the scenes to execute plans, the vision of the Eagles, direction of the Lions, and relational harmony of the Doves will remain incomplete. Just as a marriage cannot survive on love alone without diligent effort, a ministry cannot thrive without dedicated workers who ensure that plans are executed and the foundation remains strong. However, a team of only Ants may lack direction and vision, just as a marriage with two highly task-driven partners may struggle with a deeper emotional connection or long-term vision. A healthy marriage and a successful ministry both require Ants who build but also a balance of leaders who bring vision, authority, and relational wisdom to the table.

THE DOVE: PEACEFUL SYNERGY AND EMOTIONAL UNDERSTANDING

Marriage is more than just shared responsibilities; it requires emotional compatibility and peace. In the same way, the Dove represents unity and understanding in leadership. Premarital counseling fosters self-awareness in this area by helping individuals assess their emotional needs, love languages, and capacity for compromise. Understanding one's own temperament and that of a partner is crucial to maintaining harmony, just as effective leadership depends on emotional intelligence and relational balance.

The Dove of the LEAD Model is a powerful symbol for determining how a couple will handle peacekeeping, emotional connection, and relational harmony in their marriage. The Dove represents compassion, wisdom, and the ability to foster unity, which are essential traits for maintaining a strong and emotionally secure relationship. A couple that embodies the Dove's qualities will prioritize understanding, communication, and emotional support, ensuring that conflicts are resolved with patience rather than power struggles.

The same is true in leadership team selection. A leader must recognize the necessity of Doves on a team, individuals who foster unity, mediate conflicts, and ensure relational health among members. Without Doves, teams become task-driven and vision-heavy but lack the glue that keeps people emotionally invested and aligned. A thriving marriage and an effective ministry both need Doves to bring peace but also Lions to lead, Eagles to see ahead, and Ants to get the work done.

In essence, premarital counseling is a mirror of how leadership teams should function. Using the LEAD Model as a guide, couples can gain deeper insight into their leadership potential (Lion), relational wisdom (Eagle), work ethic (Ant), and emotional harmony (Dove). By doing so, they set the foundation for personal and professional relationships that are built on mutual understanding, shared vision, and a commitment to growing together. In other words, they are equally yoked. This alignment ensures that they are not just walking side by side but moving in the same direction with unity and purpose. Just as two oxen must be evenly matched to plow effectively, strong relationships must be equally aligned to function properly. It is the leader's responsibility to ensure that the ministries they construct are partnerships wherein burdens are shared, strengths are amplified, and challenges are tackled together, fostering a bond that is both resilient and deeply rooted in faith.

SIGNS OF BEING UNEQUALLY YOKED

As our church began to flourish, so did the demands of our media production department. The growth of our congregation and the increasing expectation for immediate, engaging, and spiritually uplifting media presented both exciting opportunities and unpredictable challenges. We soon discovered that expanding our media team was not just about adding skilled hands to our production; it was about cultivating a cohesive spirit that could resonate with the mission and core values of our church.

In the early days of our media production department, our responsibilities were straightforward. However, as the congregation grew, the complexity of our services increased dramatically. We needed a team that could:

- **Answer online prayer requests in real-time:** Each prayer request was a sacred opportunity to connect with our community, and timely responses could mean the difference between a moment of divine comfort and a missed opportunity for healing and discipleship.
- **Display scriptures at pivotal moments:** Whether in moments of reflection or during dynamic sermons, bringing up the right scripture at the right time was essential to

amplify our message. I discovered that our church members, like most today, are visual and can glean more from the message when there is a visual connected to the audible word. Therefore, creating compelling video slides and graphics was vital. Our services began incorporating multimedia elements that not only communicated our message but also captured the hearts of our viewers.

Each of these tasks required a unique blend of technical skill and spiritual sensitivity. I knew that to meet these challenges, we had to recruit a team of individuals who excelled in their respective fields, people who could manage both the technical demands of production and the delicate nature of ministry work. I learned, though, that building a skilled team to get through a Sunday service was much easier than building a team that would last because they liked working together.

Without considering the process of self-assessment, armed only with our clearly defined needs, I reached out to professionals with a reputation for excellence in digital media, graphic design, and live production. I was confident that their technical expertise would merge into a powerhouse capable of elevating our digital ministry to new heights. The initial promise was immense; here were talented individuals, each an expert in his or her domain, ready to serve the mission of the ministry.

However, as we began to work together, a crucial issue emerged: while the technical skills were undeniable, the team lacked the unity necessary for seamless collaboration. The media team, built on individual brilliance, struggled with interpersonal dynamics. Communication lines became blurred, and without a shared framework for teamwork, friction quickly escalated.

> *Talent alone does not guarantee success; it must be harnessed within a framework of mutual accountability and shared purpose.*

The most challenging aspect was not the technical demands of our digital tasks but rather the dynamics between team members. One individual in particular believed that his expertise placed him above the usual chain of command. This person was unwilling to take orders from anyone but me, undermining the structure we had painstakingly built. His refusal to collaborate on an equal footing led to tensions that rippled through the entire team, causing delays and diluting our collective mission.

This conflict was not just about authority; it was a symptom of a deeper challenge in team integration. When a group of highly talented individuals operates without mutual respect and clear communication, the result can be a fractured team rather than a unified department. The situation underscored an important leadership lesson: talent alone does not guarantee success; it must be harnessed within a framework of mutual accountability and shared purpose.

Faced with these internal challenges, I turned to the principles of the LEAD Model, a framework built on clear communication, empathy, accountability, and decisive action. The model taught me that effective leadership is about more than directing tasks; it's about fostering an environment where each member understands their role and feels genuinely valued.

Using the LEAD Model, I recognized that this individual was a Lion—a strong-willed, authoritative leader who was confident in his own abilities but struggled with team collaboration. Lions naturally take charge and often prefer direct leadership interactions, sometimes seeing peers as obstacles rather than allies. In this case, the challenge wasn't his capability but his reluctance to work within the team dynamic. Rather than replacing him, I knew the key was to retrain and help him refine his leadership style to be more effective in a collaborative environment.

The retraining process involved helping the Lion understand the value of the other team members—the Eagles' vision, the Ants' execution, and the Doves' ability to foster and maintain relational harmony. I reinforced that true leadership isn't about operating in isolation but about empowering others to succeed alongside you. I set clear expectations for teamwork, encouraged strategic delegation, and positioned him in scenarios where he had to rely on others to accomplish key tasks. Over time, he began to see that his strength as a leader wasn't diminished by collaboration; it was actually enhanced by leveraging the gifts of those around him. By redirecting his natural leadership energy rather than suppressing it, I was able to transform his mindset from solo leadership to team leadership, ensuring that he remained a valuable and cooperative asset to our ministry.

If you are dealing with a leadership style whose strengths are becoming weaknesses, you can follow the same key steps that I took to resolve this issue:

1) **Clarified roles and responsibilities:** I redefined each team member's responsibilities and set clear boundaries on decision-making. This clarity helped reduce overlaps and

conflicts, ensuring that everyone knew exactly what was expected of them.

2) **Established a unified vision:** I took time to communicate the broader vision of our digital ministry. By emphasizing that every task—from answering prayer requests to creating video slides—contributed to a larger mission, I fostered a sense of shared purpose among the team members.

3) **Opened communication channels:** I introduced regular team meetings and one-on-one check-ins. These forums provided space for feedback, allowed conflicts to be addressed early and helped everyone align on our common goals.

4) **Resolved conflicts decisively:** When conflicts arose, I intervened promptly, mediating discussions, reiterating the importance of collaboration, and reminding the team of the core values of our church: love, trust, and discipleship. Every team member needed to understand that no one person's expertise was above the collective mission.

By applying these strategies, we slowly began to transform a disjointed group into a more harmonious team. While the process was neither immediate nor easy, it was a powerful lesson in leadership and the importance of unity.

> *Leadership is as much about managing people and fostering unity as it is about technical or operational expertise.*

The journey of building our media production department taught me several invaluable lessons. First, I learned that the leaders should always demand unity over individualism. In any mission-driven environment, especially one as sensitive as a church's digital ministry, the collective vision must always trump individual egos. I learned that clear communication is crucial. Ambiguity and miscommunication can quickly derail even the most technically competent teams. Clear, consistent dialogue is essential. As pastors, we must demand and demonstrate adaptability in leadership. No leadership model is perfect out of the box. The challenges we faced required me to adapt, refine my approach, and sometimes make tough decisions to keep the mission on track and the ministry moving forward. I learned to make sure each team member felt valued and needed. A shared mission helped the team see beyond personal differences and focus on the common goal of serving our community.

Ultimately, the challenges within our media production department underscored a fundamental truth: leadership is as much about managing people and fostering unity as it is about technical or operational expertise. Pastors should know that the LEAD Model is not a static set of instructions but a living framework that evolves with each new challenge. Our experience reaffirmed that a leader's true strength lies in the ability to inspire, equip, and empower a diverse team toward a shared vision, even when the road is rocky.

As we continue to grow and adapt, the lessons learned from that tumultuous period remain at the heart of our mission. They serve as a constant reminder that while talent is essential, it is the power of collective purpose and disciplined leadership that truly drives lasting impact and lasting success.

THE CONSEQUENCES OF AN UNEQUALLY YOKED RELATIONSHIP

Even when both individuals are saved, they may still be unequally yoked if:

- **They have nothing in common**: Shared faith is foundational, but it is not enough. If two people have different visions, interests, or values, they will struggle to find unity.
- **They have different levels of commitment**: One person may be more spiritually mature, more disciplined, or more committed to their purpose than the other, causing friction.
- **They have conflicting goals**: When one person is focused on God's kingdom and the other is distracted by worldly pursuits, their partnership becomes strained. Just as unequally yoked oxen move in circles, mismatched relationships can lead to stagnation instead of growth. Differences in values or priorities can create tension and misunderstandings that will ultimately lead to more stress experienced by the pastor.

To be equally yoked, both individuals must align their goals. Shared vision and purpose are essential for effective collaboration. This requires open communication and a commitment to work toward the same objectives. Both individuals must be willing to grow spiritually and emotionally, ensuring that one does not carry the burden alone.

Take time to assess your relationships and partnerships. Are you equally yoked with the people you're walking alongside?

Ask yourself: Do we share common goals and values? Are we moving forward together, or are we stuck in a cycle of conflict and frustration? How can I contribute to creating a balanced and harmonious relationship?

If you recognize that you are unequally yoked in any area of your life or your ministry, it's not too late to make changes. Seek God's wisdom and guidance to strengthen the relationship. Communicate openly about your differences and work toward unity. If the relationship or ministerial team cannot be realigned, prayerfully consider whether it is time to retrain, reassign, or remove. Be intentional about forming relationships with people who share your vision and values.

THE BOTTOM LINE

Being equally yoked is about more than shared faith; it's about alignment in purpose, priorities, and progress. When relationships are built on mutual respect, shared goals, and a commitment to growth, they become powerful vehicles for building your ministry, accomplishing God's work, and fulfilling your earthly assignment. Take the time to evaluate your yokes, ensuring they propel you forward rather than hold you back.

If a pastor were to ask me, "Luke, how do I select team members who are equally yoked?", I would begin by introducing the idea that equal yoking in leadership is not about uniformity but about balance. Just as in marriage, where two people must be aligned in purpose while complementing each other's strengths, a leadership team must be a well-balanced blend of different leadership styles to function effectively. The key is understanding not only the strengths and weaknesses of potential team members but also the type of leader you are, as that influences how you build your team.

Using the LEAD Model, I would also explain that a pastor cannot build a successful team by only surrounding themselves with leaders who think, act, and lead the same way they do. For a team to be equally yoked, it must have a healthy combination of Lions, Eagles, Ants, and Doves. Too many Lions can lead to power struggles, too many Eagles may result in vision without execution, too many Ants can focus on work without direction, and too many Doves might prioritize relationships over decisions.

A pastor must first assess their own leadership style, whether they naturally lead as a Lion (authority), Eagle (visionary), Ant (worker), or Dove (peacemaker), so that they can select a team that balances out their strengths and fills in their gaps. Equal yoking in leadership means strategically placing individuals where their strengths can complement rather than compete with one another, creating a team that is both spiritually and functionally aligned.

CHAPTER 3

THE FEARLESS LEADER

A Lion's Roar

WHILE SERVING IN A PROMINENT leadership role at a rapidly growing ministry, I was honored to be part of a church that was building the people who were building the church. I watched as the pastor worked tirelessly to assemble a core leadership team, one that could help him manage the growth and serve the congregation effectively.

As I observed his selections, I noticed a pattern: he was primarily surrounding himself with bold, confident, and results-driven leaders—Lions. These individuals had a commanding presence, took charge easily, and executed the pastor's vision with strength and determination. At first, his selections appeared to be wise decisions. After all, Lions bring authority, courage, and a no-nonsense approach to leadership, all qualities that are essential for managing expansion and keeping the ministry moving forward.

However, over time, I became deeply concerned about their interactions with members. The problem wasn't their strength;

it was their lack of balance. Lions are natural rulers, but without accountability and guidance, their leadership can easily become domineering rather than empowering. The very qualities that made them effective in decision-making and structure also made them intimidating and unapproachable to the congregation. Instead of nurturing and guiding the sheep, these Lions were ruling over them, enforcing authority rather than showing care.

What troubled me most was that the pastor had no idea what was happening. He trusted his core team wholeheartedly, assuming they were leading with the same compassion and understanding that he had for the people. But in reality, the very members that he was trying to serve were struggling under the weight of the leaders that he assigned.

> *Leadership is not just about power. It's about stewardship.*

Thinking on this experience brought the LEAD Model into focus for me. A healthy, thriving ministry cannot be built on one leadership style alone. While Lions bring strength and direction, they work best when balanced with other leadership styles:
- Visionary leaders who see beyond the present and guide the ministry with wisdom and foresight.
- Hardworking, dedicated individuals who focus on serving with diligence and consistency.

- Nurturing, compassionate leaders who care for the people and ensure they feel valued and heard.

Had the pastor intentionally balanced his leadership team with all four types of leadership traits, the ministry would have been both strong and sustainable. Instead, with too many Lions, the congregation was left feeling ruled instead of led, managed instead of ministered to. Many members left the church, stating that they didn't feel valued, protected, or that their voices were being heard. They didn't blame the pastor's leadership team for how they felt; they blamed the pastor.

This experience opened my eyes to a vital truth: leadership is not just about power. It's about stewardship. A shepherd must not only appoint leaders, but he must also watch over the flock to ensure they are being led with both strength and grace.

A well-balanced team, where each leader operates in their God-given strengths, creates a ministry that is both powerful and nurturing, structured yet compassionate, growing yet grounded.

This experience highlights a common leadership challenge: how does the pastor build a team with strong, dominant leaders while ensuring they serve with compassion and wisdom?

The pastor, in his zeal to build a powerful leadership team, surrounded himself with Lions—leaders who were bold, authoritative, and driven—but they lacked the gentleness and sensitivity needed to care for the congregation, the sheep.

The Bible speaks of this in Ezekiel 34:2 and 4: "Woe to you shepherds of Israel who only take care of yourselves! Should not shepherds take care of the flock? . . . You have ruled them harshly and brutally."

Also, in John 10:11-13, Jesus contrasts the Good Shepherd (who truly cares for the sheep) with the hired hand (who does not).

This is a powerful example of why leadership balance is crucial and how even well-meaning pastors can unknowingly allow strong but unchecked leaders to harm the very people they are called to serve.

This passage paints a vivid picture of the core characteristics of a Lion:

> *"Judah, your brothers will praise you;*
> *your hand will be on the neck of your enemies;*
> *your father's sons will bow down to you.*
> *You are a lion's cub, Judah;*
> *you return from the prey, my son.*
> *Like a lion he crouches and lies down,*
> *like a lioness—who dares to rouse him?*
> *The scepter will not depart from Judah,*
> *nor the ruler's staff from between his feet,*
> *until he to whom it belongs shall come*
> *and the obedience of the nations shall be his.*
> *He will tether his donkey to a vine,*
> *his colt to the choicest branch;*
> *he will wash his garments in wine,*
> *his robes in the blood of grapes.*
> *His eyes will be darker than wine,*
> *his teeth whiter than milk."*
> —Genesis 49:8-12

Judah is depicted as a lion, embodying strength, authority, and leadership. The lion is not only a symbol of power but also of order, balance, and purpose. These characteristics reflect the qualities of a true leader—one who leads with both courage and wisdom.

In the LEAD Model, the Lion represents a strong, bold, and decisive leader, someone who naturally takes charge and thrives in positions of authority. To identify the Lion personality in a ministry setting, a pastor should look for the following core characteristics:

1) **They thrive in structured environments where expectations and boundaries are clear.** They desire order and will work to establish it wherever chaos exists. Their roar often serves as a demand for alignment and peace rather than a call to conflict.
2) **Their drive is fueled by achieving goals and reaching milestones.** They measure their progress through accomplishments and seek to overcome challenges to ensure success.
3) **They naturally step into leadership roles.** They possess an innate ability to guide and inspire others, taking charge when necessary and ensuring that the group moves forward. Challenges do not intimidate lions; they embrace them as opportunities for growth and victory. Their strength and determination are most evident in adversity.
4) **They do not engage in conflict for the sake of conflict.** Instead, they fight to restore peace and order, ensuring that harmony prevails in their environment.
5) **They are doers.** They do not wait idly for change but take decisive steps to address problems and seize opportunities.

6) **They communicate clearly and expect the same from others.** They are not afraid to demand excellence. They often push those around them to reach their full potential.
7) **Their willpower is unmatched.** Once they set their sights on a goal, they are relentless in pursuing it. Their drive inspires others to keep going even in difficult times.
8) **They move quickly and expect others to keep up.** Their limited patience can sometimes make them appear curt, but it stems from their urgency to achieve results. While lions may come across as uncaring, this is often a misconception. Their focus on goals can sometimes overshadow their ability to express empathy openly.
9) **They love being around individuals who challenge them intellectually and spiritually.** They are drawn to people who bring value and wisdom into their lives. It's important to note that in spite of their confidence, their strength can make them wary of those who might exploit it. They guard themselves against manipulation and strive to maintain control over their circumstances.
10) **Lions enjoy the company of others but also value their personal space.** They want you to be around, but they also want you to know when it's time to leave. If lions feel they are not growing under someone else's leadership, they will step into the leadership role themselves. They are committed to progress and will not tolerate stagnation.

LESSONS FROM THE LION

The Lion's characteristics are a blueprint for effective leadership and personal growth. Whether in ministry, family, or professional settings, identifying these traits can help you lead the Lion with strength, wisdom, and purpose. Let the Lion of Judah be your example as you strive to bring order, inspire growth, and create harmony in your ministry and personal life.

Let's take a look at the Lion's greatest strengths.

Boldness and Confidence

When it comes to boldness and confidence, the Lion leadership style stands out as a clear example:

- They exude confidence and are not afraid to take risks.
- They are comfortable making tough decisions, even in high-pressure situations.
- Their presence is often commanding, and people naturally follow them.
- They are fearless and move with conviction, even in the face of danger. A lion-like leader stands firm in adversity.

Scriptures:

Proverbs 28:1: *"The wicked flee when no one pursues, but the righteous are bold as a lion."*

Joshua 1:9: *"Have I not commanded you? Be strong and courageous. Do not be afraid; do not be discouraged, for the LORD your God will be with you wherever you go."*

Proverbs 28:1 emphasizes the inner boldness that comes from righteous character, and Joshua 1:9 emphasizes the outward confidence that comes from divine commissioning. Together, they show that the Lion is both internally grounded and externally empowered. That combination makes the Lion not just brave but biblically qualified to lead.

Strategic Leaders

Lions lead with vision, strength, and a natural sense of authority that moves ministries forward with purpose:

- They have a clear concept for the future and inspire others to work toward it.
- They are strategic thinkers who set ambitious goals and expect results.
- They are often the ones proposing big ideas and pushing the ministry forward.
- They are known as the king of the jungle, symbolizing dominion and natural leadership.
- They take charge with authority and direction.

Scriptures:

Genesis 49:9-10 (ESV): *"Judah is a lion's cub; from the prey, my son, you have gone up. . . . The scepter shall not depart from Judah, nor the ruler's staff from between his feet."*

Matthew 28:18: *"Then Jesus came to them and said, 'All authority in heaven and on earth has been given to me.'"*

The Lion isn't just instinctively bold; he is divinely positioned, spiritually commissioned, and strategically effective.

Authority and Influence

When it comes to leading with confidence and commanding respect, lion-like leaders instinctively rise to the occasion:

- They naturally assume leadership roles, even in group settings.
- They are assertive and persuasive, often able to rally people around a cause.
- They do not shy away from responsibility and take charge when needed.
- They possess physical and mental strength, enabling them to overcome challenges. Spiritual leaders need inner strength to endure.

Scriptures:

Isaiah 40:31 (NKJV): *"But those who wait on the LORD Shall renew their strength; They shall mount up with wings like eagles, They shall run and not be weary, They shall walk and not faint."*

Philippians 4:13 (NKJV): *"I can do all things through Christ who strengthens me."*

The source of a Lion's strength doesn't come only from natural dominance but from God-given endurance and spiritual empowerment, which is the foundation of lasting authority and kingdom influence.

Strong Work Ethic and Determination

Lions are naturally hard workers who don't easily take no for an answer. This kind of leader stands out:

- They are goal-driven and work tirelessly to accomplish their objectives.
- They do not back down from challenges and face obstacles head-on.
- They expect excellence from themselves and others.

- They face opposition head-on, standing firm against spiritual and earthly opposition.

Scriptures:

2 Samuel 17:10 (ESV): *"Then even the valiant man, whose heart is like the heart of a lion, will utterly melt."*
Ephesians 6:11: *"Put on the full armor of God, so that you can take your stand against the devil's schemes."*

The Lion is not just courageous but a disciplined warrior, determined, prepared, and consistently engaged in the work and warfare of leadership.

Decisiveness and Problem-Solving Ability

Lions are marked by their ability to act quickly, trust their instincts, and persist through obstacles:

- They do not hesitate in decision-making; they trust their instincts.
- They are problem-solvers who tackle issues quickly and efficiently.
- They prefer action over prolonged discussion.
- They do not give up easily when pursuing prey, but they persist in their calling despite hardships.

Scriptures:

Hebrews 12:1: *"Let us run with perseverance the race marked out for us."*
Galatians 6:9: *"Let us not become weary in doing good, for at the proper time we will reap a harvest if we do not give up."*

The Lion not only makes sharp decisions but also solves problems through spiritual perseverance and clarity of purpose.

Independence and Self-Reliance

Lions are naturally self-directed and carry a strong sense of personal responsibility:

- They are highly independent and prefer to lead rather than follow.
- They do not easily rely on others for direction or validation.
- They take ownership of their actions and responsibilities.

Scriptures:

Mark 10:42-45: *"Jesus called them together and said, 'You know that those who are regarded as rulers of the Gentiles lord it over them. . . . Not so with you. Instead, whoever wants to become great among you must be your servant.'"*

1 Peter 5:2-3: *"Be shepherds of God's flock that is under your care, watching over them—not because you must, but because you are willing, as God wants you to be."*

Lions stand firm in their calling, lead from within, and serve with humble independence grounded in purpose—not pride. Leadership is not about oppression but about rightful authority. Good leaders lead with strength—not arrogance.

Protective Nature

Lions carry a fierce sense of responsibility for those under their care. For example:

- They defend their team, congregation, and mission with great passion.
- They stand up for what they believe is right, even in the face of opposition.
- They are loyal to those they lead but expect loyalty in return.

- They protect their pride. They look after their people, ensuring they are safe and well-guided.

Scriptures:
John 10:11: *"I am the good shepherd. The good shepherd lays down his life for the sheep."*
Nehemiah 4:14: *"Don't be afraid of them. Remember the Lord, who is great and awesome, and fight for your families, your sons and your daughters, your wives and your homes."*

The Lion doesn't just lead with strength but with a fierce, sacrificial commitment to protecting their people, purpose, and place of responsibility.

GUIDING A LION PERSONALITY

While Lions are great leaders and have great personalities, they are also lifelong learners. The best way to lead a lion is to:

- Encourage them to **balance boldness with humility,** ensuring they lead with love.
- Help them recognize the **value of teamwork** and listening to others.
- Remind them that **gentleness is not weakness but strength under control,** and great leaders use their strengths to empower others.
- Challenge them to **develop patience and empathy,** especially with different personality types, because this does not come naturally to them.

A Lion personality is a powerful asset to any ministry when guided correctly. By recognizing these characteristics and providing spiritual mentorship, a pastor can ensure that Lions lead effectively and reflect Christ's leadership style—bold yet compassionate. The Bible says in Galatians 5:22-23: "But the fruit of the Spirit is love, joy, peace, forbearance, kindness, goodness, faithfulness, gentleness and self-control. Against such things there is no law."

> *It's important to accept a Lion for who they are rather than trying to change their personality.*

The Lion's strong, decisive, and driven traits can be balanced by combining them with the fruit of the Spirit. The Lion's natural leadership and determination can be even more effective when paired with love, patience, and sensitivity. Patience is one of the most challenging yet transformative fruits of the Spirit for a Lion to cultivate. Lions are naturally fast-paced and action-oriented, often becoming frustrated with delays or inefficiency. However, by showing patience, they can:

- Build stronger relationships with those who move at a different pace.
- Avoid discouraging others who may feel overwhelmed by their intensity.
- Model Christ's example of forbearance, which inspires others to grow.

Lions are often direct and focused on results, which can make them appear insensitive. By developing sensitivity, they can:
- Better understand the needs and emotions of those they lead.
- Create an environment where people feel valued and supported.
- Foster trust and deepen their connections with others.

Lions tend to trust their instincts and make decisions quickly, which can sometimes lead them to dismiss other perspectives. Growth in this area involves:
- Actively listening to others and showing that their opinions are valued.
- Recognizing that collaboration often leads to better solutions.
- Demonstrating humility by being open to learning from others.

HOW TO ENGAGE A LION LEADER

Understanding how to relate to a Lion is essential for fostering healthy relationships and effective collaboration. Here are practical tips:

1) **Earn their trust.** A Lion will only allow themselves to be trained or tamed by someone they trust. Building trust requires consistency, integrity, and respect. Without trust, a Lion will keep their emotional distance and remain guarded.

2) **Get to the point.** Lions appreciate direct communication. When speaking with a lion, avoid lengthy explanations or unnecessary details. Be clear, concise, and focused, or risk losing their attention (or hearing them growl).

3) **Come with solutions.** Never approach a lion with just a problem; always bring a solution. Lions value order and decisiveness, so presenting potential solutions demonstrates respect for their time and focus.
4) **Disappoint at a manageable rate.** Lions are not out to break spirits, but they are clear about their expectations. They may disappoint people by setting firm boundaries or enforcing standards, but they aim to do so in a way that others can understand and learn from.

FINAL THOUGHTS ON LEADING LIONS

Beneath the Lion's strength and commanding presence lies a tender heart. The Lion is really a lamb. If you take the time to earn their trust and truly know them, you will discover that they are fiercely loyal and willing to sacrifice for those they care about. A Lion will die for you if they believe in you.

It's important to accept a Lion for who they are rather than trying to change their personality. Instead, focus on helping them channel their strengths in ways that align with God's purpose and plan. Growth doesn't mean losing their unique qualities but refining them to reflect the fruit of the Spirit.

Lions bring strength, determination, and leadership to any situation. By growing in patience, sensitivity, and humility, they can lead with greater impact and grace. Understanding how to handle a Lion, earn their trust, communicate effectively, and respect their personality will create an environment where both the Lion and those around them can thrive. The balance of strength and gentleness, modeled after Christ, transforms the Lion into a leader who not only inspires but also nurtures those they serve.

When dealing with a Lion, prayer is essential. Ask God for wisdom and guidance with this prayer:

> *"Lord, show me how to approach this person with humility and grace. Teach me to understand their heart and how to work with them effectively."*

CHAPTER 4

THE VISIONARY LEADER

An Eagle's-Eye Vision

While meeting with a group of young pastors, I posed three critical questions:

1) What are your strengths and areas for growth or developmental challenges?
2) Where do you envision your ministry in the next five years?
3) Do you currently have the skill set to lead your ministry to that vision?

As expected, many of the pastors identified communication, especially preaching and writing, as their greatest strengths. They all had bold visions of a thriving ministry in the next five years. Yet, many admitted they lacked the strategic skills needed to turn that vision into reality. They could see the destination but struggled to chart the course. This highlights a few key characteristics among leaders with an Eagle personality: they soar with vision but often lack the framework to execute it. Pastors whose dominant leadership style is not the Eagle need big-picture visionaries on their team.

These pastors could write the vision but struggled to make it plain, a direct reflection of Habakkuk 2:2 (NKJV): "Write the vision And make *it* plain on tablets, That he may run who reads it." While God calls leaders to cast vision, He also calls them to build the structure that brings that vision to fruition.

Understanding the Eagle of the LEAD Model equips pastors to both recognize and cultivate visionary leadership in themselves and others. The Eagle represents a leader with vision, strategy, and foresight, someone who not only sees the destination but also discerns the path to get there. Pastors who identify as Eagles must ask themselves, "Do I embody these traits?" If so, they must harness their gifting to build strategic plans, delegate with wisdom, and lead their teams toward fulfilling God-given visions. If not, it becomes essential to learn how to identify Eagle traits in team members who naturally possess sharp discernment, long-range thinking, and the ability to strategize. By mentoring these individuals, pastors can develop a leadership team that complements their strengths and expands the reach of their ministry.

When pastors or other executive leaders embrace the Eagle mindset, whether living it out or empowering others to do so, they move beyond mere inspiration to powerful execution, turning God-given dreams into ministries that make a lasting impact.

As you consider the Eagle, take a moment to reflect: how closely does this leadership style mirror your own? Do you naturally operate with vision, foresight, and strategic thinking? Or do you recognize these traits more clearly in someone on your team? Think about the individuals you serve alongside who consistently see the bigger picture, anticipate what's ahead, and help steer the ministry with clarity and direction. Start asking yourself, *Who am I working with?* Begin identifying the Eagles in your leadership circle, those who soar above the chaos to gain perspective and help guide others with confidence. The more clearly you can recognize this trait, the better equipped you'll be to position your team members where they can truly thrive and flourish. As we continue exploring the other leadership types in the LEAD Model, you'll be able to assess whether you have a balanced team and, if not, how to build one that functions with unity, purpose, and kingdom impact.

THE EAGLE'S VISION: UNLOCKING THE TRAITS OF A FUTURE-FOCUSED LEADER

The Eagle represents a visionary leader, someone who sees the possibility of a thing, thinks strategically, and soars above challenges with clarity and purpose. In the LEAD Model, the Eagle represents vision, foresight, and adaptability. These traits distinguish Eagles as visionary leaders who are proactive, discerning, and focused. Eagles are renowned for their extraordinary vision. They can see prey from miles away, allowing them to anticipate and plan their next move with precision.

Let's explore the LEAD Model traits of a leader who possesses the DNA of an Eagle. Below are their key characteristics, along with corresponding Bible verses that highlight these traits.

Visionary Leadership

They see beyond the present.

Eagle-minded leaders can see far ahead and set clear goals for the future. They understand where they are going and can articulate that vision to others. Without clear vision, people wander aimlessly, but a leader with the Eagle mindset ensures that the path forward is well-defined.

Proverbs 29:18 (KJV): "Where *there is* no vision, the people perish: but he that keepeth the law, happy is he."

Strategic Thinking

They plan for success.

Eagles don't just see the future; they prepare for it by anticipating challenges and developing strategies to overcome them. They understand that true leadership requires careful planning; therefore, Eagles assess resources, strengths, and weaknesses before taking action.

Luke 14:28 (author paraphrase): "For which of you intending to build a tower, does not sit down first and count the cost, whether he has enough to finish it?"

High Standards and Excellence

They soar above mediocrity.

Eagles don't settle for average; they aim for greatness and push others to do the same. They lead with integrity and expect excellence from those on their team. Leaders with an Eagle personality pursue excellence in all areas, knowing that their work is not only a reflection of themselves, their ministry, and their church, but, ultimately, it reflects God's glory.

Colossians 3:23 (KJV): "And whatsoever ye do, do it heartily, as to the Lord, and not unto men."

Courage and Confidence

They take calculated risks and empower others.

Eagles are not afraid to fly alone or face storms head-on. They embrace challenges and trust in God's strength. They understand that bold leadership requires stepping out in faith, unshaken by fear or opposition. But they also understand that they can't accomplish great things alone. They invest in others, training them to rise to their full potential. They are wise leaders who know how to develop, delegate, and empower others to lead effectively.

Second Timothy 1:7 (KJV): "For God hath not given us the spirit of fear; but of power, and of love, and of a sound mind."

Patience and Renewal

They rest and wait on God.

Eagles know when to soar and when to rest. They find their strength in God, not in their own abilities. Experience has taught them that they cannot always be in motion; they must take time to rest and renew their strength through prayer and reliance on God.

Isaiah 40:3 (KJV): "But they that wait upon the LORD shall renew *their* strength; they shall mount up with wings as eagles; they shall run, and not be weary; *and* they shall walk, and not faint."

Consider the Big Picture

They think long-term.

Eagles often focus on long-term goals and strategies, knowing what needs to be done but understanding they may not always be the ones to execute every detail. For example, a basketball coach envisions the team's success and creates the framework for victory, but the players execute the plays.

Eagles look ahead, often planning for years into the future. They are futuristic thinkers. Much like an eagle spotting a rabbit three miles away, these leaders foresee opportunities and challenges years ahead and begin planning accordingly. They understand the importance of preparing for what's next, ensuring their vision aligns with sustainable growth and development.

Eagles are built to endure storms and emerge stronger. They have a protective membrane over their eyes that allows them to fly through storms and see clearly when others cannot. For an Eagle-minded leader, this resilience translates into:

1) **Special discernment and natural problem-solving:** They remain attentive and focused, even in turbulent times. After weathering storms, their clarity of vision improves. Eagles rise above challenges, maintaining a positive outlook and looking for solutions to improve situations. While others may falter in difficult circumstances, Eagles perform best when conditions are favorable and can thrive even when times are tough.

   Eagles are natural problem solvers, always seeking ways to improve and organize. Unlike the Lion, who may leave problems unresolved, Eagles fix the unorganized. They approach problems with a positive mindset, thinking of ways to make things better. For example, rather than complaining about a broken situation, they'll suggest, "It won't look that bad if we fix it this way."

2) **Relational strength and resilience:** Eagles avoid unnecessary drama and focus on finding ways to rise above

challenges. They bring stability and focus to a team, ensuring progress even during uncertainty. Eagles value relationships and thrive in environments where they can engage with others. Contrary to traditional thought, Eagles are outgoing and active and naturally attract others. People want to be around them, and their behavior sets the tone for others. They need opportunities to engage and get involved. They dislike monotony. Being stuck in a routine can frustrate them.

3) **Wired for loyalty, wounded by criticism:** Eagles are deeply loyal, sometimes to a fault. While Lions may only remain loyal to those who reciprocate, Eagles tend to stick by people even when it's not deserved. Eagles care deeply about how they are perceived. This trait makes them effective influencers but also vulnerable to criticism. They care about what others think, often taking breakups or rejections personally. A Lion may brush it off and move on, but an Eagle will reflect, wondering, Was it me? Eagles take pride in their appearance and their reputation. Criticism can weigh on them and impact their confidence.

4) **Strategic stillness and patience that pays off:** In the wild, Eagles are masters of patience, demonstrating an unwavering ability to wait for the right moment before making their move. Unlike Lions, which rely on speed and strength to secure immediate results, Eagles understand that timing and persistence often lead to greater rewards. They do not rush into action but instead observe their surroundings carefully, ensuring that their efforts are both strategic and effective. This ability to exercise patience and discernment

is a powerful leadership trait, one that allows great leaders to make wise decisions rather than being driven by urgency or impulse.

5) **The courage to decide:** Eagles are also known for their decisiveness; when they lock onto a target, they strike with precision and confidence. In leadership, this translates to bold decision-making and a commitment to excellence.

As we explore the leadership lessons from Eagles, we will uncover the characteristics that define this style and learn how to leverage their remarkable ability to inspire others to reach their fullest potential. Here are some leadership keys that will make your interaction with an Eagle constructive.

PARTNERING WITH VISIONARIES

Working alongside an Eagle requires more than just admiration for their ideas—it demands intentional collaboration. To bring out their best, leaders must create space for vision to flourish while offering the support and trust that fuels their momentum. Here are some best practices for working with an Eagle.

Encourage Visionary Thinking

Create an environment that nurtures long-term planning and strategic foresight, allowing the Eagle to soar with big-picture ideas. They thrive in an environment that celebrates their ingenuity and sagacity.

Build Trusting Relationships

Pastors can cultivate trust and loyalty within their ministry teams by consistently affirming the value each person brings and by fostering a culture of collaboration. Helping team members see the role of unity in achieving shared goals strengthens the foundation of effective leadership. When it comes to Eagles and Lions, one of the most powerful ways to show appreciation is through trust and autonomy. These leaders thrive when they are empowered with independence and given the freedom to operate within their strengths.

One of the most important things a pastor can do to lead well is to recognize that every leader on the team is wired differently. Building strong relationships starts with understanding what each personality type values and then meeting them there. Pastors foster trust and loyalty when they consistently show that they value each team member's unique contributions and highlight the importance of teamwork in achieving lasting success.

With Eagles and Lions, appreciation looks like trust and empowerment. These leaders are fueled by independence, vision, and responsibility. They thrive when they know you believe in their ability to make decisions and lead without micromanagement. Giving them room to operate in their strengths is one of the most powerful ways to build a lasting relationship.

However, recognizing these differences will help you build stronger, more intentional relationships with every member of your team, allowing each one to flourish while working together for a greater kingdom purpose.

Model Patience and Discernment

An Eagle brings wisdom in timing and decision-making, ensuring that every action aligns with the greater vision. Their patience and discernment help guide the ministry with strategic insight, avoiding hasty choices while seizing the right opportunities for growth.

By applying these principles, you can create a leadership dynamic that maximizes the strengths of an Eagle personality while fostering a thriving and motivated team.

THROUGH THE EYES OF AN EAGLE: AREAS OF GROWTH

In the LEAD Model, the Eagle embodies vision, resilience, and proactive leadership, qualities that fuel momentum, inspire teams, and often propel ministries forward. Eagles have the unique ability to see what's ahead and chart a path to get there. However, like any strength, these traits can present challenges when not tempered by self-awareness, humility, and flexibility. The greatest growth opportunities for Eagles often come through learning to soften intensity, welcome collaboration, and adapt to the realities of the people and resources around them. Sometimes, those working within the team—rather than the person who's over the team—know what is best for the team.

This was a major area of growth for me personally. Coming from an executive position within the federal government, I was trained to hear the objectives from leadership and immediately formulate an actionable strategy for my region. My world revolved around results. I was used to working with people who simply figured out how to get it done, no matter the obstacles.

However, when I transitioned into the role of senior pastor, I quickly discovered that ministry leadership required a different approach. I still had vision and drive, but now I was working with volunteers, limited budgets, and team members with varying capacities. I had to adjust to hearing, "Sorry, Pastor, we just can't do it that way. We don't have the resources, the budget, or the personnel." That was a humbling and transformative shift for me as an Eagle-eyed leader.

Eagles must learn that leadership isn't just about the destination; it's about the journey and the people who walk it with you. Growth comes when we balance our vision with compassion, our strategy with sensitivity, and our boldness with patience.

By understanding these areas for growth, both Eagles and those who work with them can foster healthier, more effective leadership dynamics. Let's explore the key areas where Eagles can develop and provide practical strategies to help them maximize their strengths while cultivating balance and flexibility in their leadership style.

LEARN TO LET GO

Eagles are known for their strength and vision, but one of their greatest challenges is knowing when to release what no longer serves them. Whether it's a past relationship, a failed decision, or an unresolved situation, holding on too tightly can prevent them from soaring to new heights. True leadership requires the wisdom to recognize when it's time to let go and trust that God's plan is unfolding.

In personal relationships, Eagles often struggle with closure, questioning whether they could have done more to salvage a relationship. Whether it's a friendship, mentorship, or leadership connection, they may replay conversations and decisions, wondering if a different approach would have changed the outcome. However, the Bible reminds us that seasons change, and not every relationship is meant to last forever.

> *When an Eagle learns to release with grace, they don't lose momentum; they actually soar higher.*

Ecclesiastes 3:1 (KJV) teaches, "To every *thing there is* a season, and a time to every purpose under the heaven." Just as an eagle sheds its old feathers to make room for new, stronger ones, leaders must also learn the discipline of release. There are times when relationships, roles, or even strategies have run their course. Letting go is not a sign of failure. It's an act of faith, trusting that God will bring fresh connections, new resources, and clearer direction aligned with the next season of the journey.

For pastors working with Eagle-type leaders, this is a critical area of discipleship. Eagles often hold tightly to people or plans because of their deep loyalty and strong sense of mission. However, this can lead to frustration or burnout when something is no longer fruitful. Pastors can guide Eagles by helping them discern when a season has ended and permitting them to release it without guilt.

Encourage your Eagles to reflect on what God might be pruning to make room for new growth. Affirm that wise release is a mark of maturity, not weakness. Use Scripture, prayer, and counsel to help them gain clarity and gently redirect their focus toward what's ahead. When an Eagle learns to release with grace, they don't lose momentum; they actually soar higher.

In ministry, Eagles also tend to dwell on mistakes, replaying their missteps instead of embracing the lessons and moving forward. This can lead to unnecessary guilt and stagnation. Yet, Scripture reminds us that failure is not final. I believe that failure is an opinion, not an absolute. Some of today's greatest creations were derived from "failure."

Philippians 3:13-14 encourages us to "[Forget] what is behind and [strain] toward what is ahead." Paul then says, "I press on toward the goal to win the prize for which God has called me heavenward in Christ Jesus."

Mistakes should be seen as stepping stones, not stumbling blocks. When an Eagle misjudges a dive or loses a catch, it does not stay grounded; it readjusts and tries again. Likewise, effective leaders must acknowledge errors, seek wisdom from them, and then release the past in order to embrace the future.

BELIEVING IN THE POWER OF FAITH

Eagles are natural strategists. They thrive on clear plans, sharp vision, and measurable outcomes. But the challenge for many

Eagle leaders lies in fully embracing the unseen—the realm of faith. Because they rely so heavily on their ability to see and plan, Eagles can sometimes struggle to trust God when the path isn't visible or the plan doesn't make sense.

This is where pastors play a crucial role. Eagles need to be reminded that while strategy is a gift, it must be coupled with surrender. Faith doesn't always follow a five-point plan. Pastors can redirect Eagles by gently challenging their need for control and encouraging them to trust God beyond what they can see. Help them understand that the greatest moves of God often begin where the roadmap ends.

Use biblical examples, like Abraham, who followed God "not knowing where he was going" (Hebrews 11:8, ESV), or Peter stepping out of the boat into uncertain waters. These stories resonate with Eagles because they show that bold and faith-filled leaders with vision still had to walk by faith, not sight.

Encourage Eagles to pray before they plan, to listen before they lead, and to rest in God's timing even when their own strategies seem more efficient. Remind them that spiritual fruit is not always immediately visible, but it is eternally impactful. True leadership is not about holding on in fear but releasing in faith, trusting that God is guiding each step.

FOCUS ON PEOPLE, NOT JUST TASKS

Although Eagles value people and relationships deeply, they are naturally task-oriented leaders who often prioritize goals over connection. Their strong sense of mission and productivity can be a great strength, but it also presents a potential weakness:

the risk of unintentionally alienating others. When an Eagle is laser-focused on outcomes, they may overlook the emotional needs of the team or fail to pause and engage on a personal level. Over time, this can create relational distance, even when that's the last thing the Eagle intends.

Interestingly, Eagles tend to be quite hard on themselves when relationships break down. They don't brush it off easily. Instead, they reflect, replay conversations, and wonder where they went wrong. This internal processing, though often hidden, can be painful, and it sometimes leads Eagles to protect themselves by placing more energy into tasks than into people. It's safer to focus on what can be accomplished than to risk the vulnerability of another relational disappointment.

That's why Eagles must be intentional about nurturing the human element. They must remind themselves that people are not just the means to a goal; they are the mission. Simple, consistent actions like checking in with team members, showing genuine interest in their lives outside of ministry or work, and offering encouragement without an agenda can go a long way. These small moments of personal connection don't just strengthen individuals; they build trust, deepen loyalty, and elevate the effectiveness of the entire team

Pastors can help Eagle leaders develop a more people-centered approach without diminishing their drive for excellence. Because Eagles are naturally wired to pursue results and operate at high levels of efficiency, they may not always realize when their focus on the mission is causing relational strain. As a pastor, you can come alongside them with both insight and accountability.

> *When Eagles learn to value people as deeply as they value outcomes, they don't lose their edge; they become transformational leaders.*

Start by affirming their strengths. Let them know that their ability to strategize and execute is invaluable, but gently remind them that leadership is not just about what gets done but how it gets done and who is brought along in the process. Create moments to reflect together on the emotional health of the team, not just the progress of the plan.

Encourage Eagles to slow down and build regular rhythms of personal connection into their leadership style. This could look like scheduled one-on-ones with team members, handwritten notes of encouragement, or even asking intentional questions before or after meetings like, "How are you doing ... really?"

You can also model this behavior for them. Show them what it looks like to lead with both vision and vulnerability. Let them see that relational investment doesn't compete with productivity; it enhances it. And when Eagles struggle with the emotional toll of relational breakdowns (which they often internalize), walk with them through healing. Help them process without shame, reminding them that God uses both strength and softness in leadership. When Eagles learn to value people as deeply as they value outcomes, they don't lose their edge; they become transformational leaders.

STAY PRESENT

Eagles have a gift for planning and thinking ahead, but this futuristic mindset can sometimes lead them to neglect the present. Their minds may constantly race with thoughts of what's next, preventing them from enjoying the moment. They can become so fixated on taking the photo for memory's sake that they miss the full joy of the moment. Eagles often miss the beauty of the here and now because they are preoccupied with what lies ahead. This can lead to unnecessary stress and burnout.

Eagles should practice mindfulness. They should take intentional breaks to savor small joys, whether it's a conversation, a meal, or a quiet moment in nature. Eagles are known for their foresight; they're always looking ahead, scanning the horizon, and mentally mapping out what's next. But this strength can also become a stumbling block. Because they are constantly anticipating outcomes and planning for future success, Eagles often struggle to stay fully present in the now. They may miss meaningful moments, overlook small wins, or find themselves overthinking interactions long after they've passed.

As a pastor, one of the greatest gifts you can give an Eagle is permission to pause. Teach them that being present is not the same as being passive; it's actually a sign of maturity and trust in God. When Eagles learn to slow down and engage with the moment, they become more effective communicators, better listeners, and more emotionally in tune with the people they lead.

Here are a few practical ways pastors can help Eagles grow in this area:

- **Model mindfulness.** Take time during meetings or gatherings to pause, breathe, pray, or celebrate something small. This demonstrates that presence is powerful.
- **Ask grounding questions.** Instead of asking, "What's next?" ask, "What's happening right now that deserves your attention?"
- **Encourage reflection without over-analysis.** Guide Eagles to process experiences with grace rather than perfectionism. Remind them they don't have to solve everything immediately.
- **Redirect them to people.** Help them see that being present with someone is often more valuable than having a solution for them.
- **Use Scripture to anchor them.** Verses like Matthew 6:34 (*"Therefore do not worry about tomorrow...."*) and Psalm 118:24 (*"This is the day the Lord has made...."*) can serve as spiritual reset points.

When Eagles learn to stop overthinking and start being, they not only find rest for themselves, but they create healthier spaces for those they lead.

EMBRACE STABILITY AMID CHANGE

Eagles thrive when they can see clearly, when the path is defined, the goal is in sight, and progress is measurable. But leadership often brings seasons where the path is uncertain, the pace is slower than desired, or God simply says, "Wait." In these moments, Eagles may feel out of alignment, restless, or even discouraged.

Pastors can help Eagle leaders grow through these times by guiding them to embrace stability not as stagnation but as a spiritual discipline. Remind them that stillness is not the absence of movement; it is the presence of trust. In God's kingdom, some of the most powerful moments happen in between the vision and the fulfillment.

Here are a few pastoral ways to support Eagles in this area:

- **Reframe the waiting.** Help them see seasons of transition as divine preparation, not wasted time. Encourage them to ask, *"What is God building in me during this pause?"*
- **Anchor them in Scripture.** Passages like Isaiah 40:31 (KJV), which says, *"They that wait upon the LORD shall renew their strength,"* remind Eagles that waiting can actually lead to greater strength and renewed vision.
- **Encourage consistency in the small things.** Stability is found in daily faithfulness, prayer, fellowship, stewardship, and service, even when the bigger picture is unclear.
- **Challenge their need for constant momentum.** Remind them that obedience is more important than outcomes. Sometimes, the most visionary thing a leader can do is stay steady in the slow season.
- **Be a voice of peace.** Speak calm into their chaos. Help them recognize that change doesn't have to mean instability when their foundation is in Christ.

When Eagles embrace stability amid change, they become not only visionary leaders but rooted leaders, anchored in God's timing and steady enough to carry others through the storm.

MANAGE EMOTIONS

Eagles experience a wide range of emotions and may struggle to keep them in check. This can lead to decisions driven by feelings rather than wisdom. Their choices may fluctuate depending on their mood, leading to inconsistency. If not managed well, their emotions can overwhelm them and those around them.

Eagles should develop emotional intelligence by identifying triggers and practicing self-regulation. They should pause before making decisions, especially in emotionally charged situations.

Because they're naturally driven and goal-oriented, Eagles may try to push past their feelings to stay productive. But unprocessed emotions don't disappear; they resurface, often in the form of frustration, burnout, or relational distance.

This is where pastors can offer meaningful guidance. Helping Eagles manage their emotions isn't about making them "less intense." It's about helping them develop emotional awareness, resilience, and balance. Here's how you can support Eagles in this area:

- **Normalize emotional processing.** Let Eagles know that feeling deeply is not a flaw; it's part of being human and spiritual. Emotions are signals, not weaknesses.
- **Create safe spaces for honest reflection.** Encourage regular check-ins or moments of vulnerability where Eagles can share struggles without fear of being judged as "less capable."
- **Teach emotional literacy.** Help them identify and name what they're feeling—frustration, disappointment, grief, fear—and bring those emotions to God in prayer.
- **Encourage Spirit-led response over reactive leadership.** Remind Eagles that self-control is a fruit of the Spirit

(Galatians 5:22-23). Slowing down to process before reacting leads to healthier outcomes.

- **Model compassion and grace.** Eagles often extend less grace to themselves than they do to others. Remind them of God's mercy and the freedom to grow at their own pace.

When pastors walk with Eagles in this area, they help them lead not only with vision but with vulnerability, strength, and empathy. Emotionally healthy Eagles become not just high-capacity leaders but whole, Spirit-led ones.

LEADING THE LEADER: PARTNERING WITH EAGLES

During my time as the deputy special agent in charge of a federal law enforcement agency, I had the unique experience of working under a leader who, like me, carried a strong Eagle personality. We were both vision-driven, confident, and passionate about strategy and results. In many ways, this alignment allowed us to work together exceptionally well. Our strengths complemented each other, and we were able to accomplish a great deal of success for the agency.

> *I had to come to terms with a powerful truth: not every good vision is a shared vision.*

But I quickly learned that when two Eagles occupy the same space, leadership requires more than vision; it requires wisdom.

There were times when my ideas didn't align with hers. And in those moments, I was faced with a choice: push for my perspective or learn to lead from the second chair. I had to come to terms with a powerful truth: not every good vision is a shared vision. And because I wasn't in the top seat, it wasn't my role to steer the ship but to help navigate it faithfully.

That shift wasn't about losing my voice or abandoning my calling; it was about learning the art of partnership. I had to surrender my ego, align with her direction, and make her vision my mission. And in doing so, I discovered something vital: great leaders don't always have to be in charge; they just have to be committed to the greater goal.

That experience taught me how to serve with strength, submit with grace, and support another Eagle without losing my own identity. It shaped the way I now work with strong leaders and helped prepare me for the seasons when others would one day support my own vision.

For those working with or leading Eagles, understanding their unique needs is crucial. Here are some tips to help them thrive:

- **Be positive and energetic:** Eagles respond well to lively environments. Bring enthusiasm to your interactions.
- **Make them laugh:** Humor helps Eagles loosen up and approach challenges with a lighter heart.
- **Let them talk:** Eagles often process their thoughts out loud. Give them space to articulate their ideas and emotions.

- **Allow for alone time:** While they enjoy engaging with others, Eagles also need moments of solitude to recharge and reflect.

Eagles are natural leaders with incredible vision and energy. By addressing these areas for growth, they can become even more effective and balanced in their leadership. Their journey to growth requires self-awareness, intentional action, and the support of those around them.

An Eagle leader is visionary, strategic, bold, and dedicated to excellence. However, to be truly effective, they must balance vision with execution, courage with wisdom, and strength with reliance on God.

If you identify as an Eagle and want to continue to grow, remember the importance of balance. Embrace the present while planning for the future. Let go of what no longer serves you. Value people as much as tasks. Manage your emotions with wisdom. In doing so, you will soar higher, with greater purpose and impact.

LESSONS FOR AN EAGLE LEADER

If you find yourself leading like an Eagle, I want you to know that as an Eagle leader, you are built to soar, to see farther, to act with courage, and to lead with clarity. But even Eagles need reminders that leadership is not sustained by strength alone. It's in trusting God to carry us, even when we don't have all the answers.

Here are three core lessons that I believe every Eagle must carry into their leadership journey:

1) **Power with humility**: Never forget that all authority comes from God. Use your influence to lift others, not to control. True power builds, protects, and honors those you lead.
2) **Vision for the future**: Stay focused on God's plan, not just your own. Seek His clarity daily and resist the pull of distractions. A clear vision guided by prayer is your greatest strength.
3) **Accountability in leadership**: Your gifts are great, but so is your responsibility. Lead with integrity, stay rooted in obedience, and remain teachable. Leadership without accountability leads to burnout, but accountability invites growth.

The Eagle's ability to soar higher than any other bird is no accident; it reflects God's call to rise above what's ordinary. In the LEAD Model, the Eagle reminds us that leadership isn't just about rising fast; it's about rising faithfully.

As Exodus 19:4 declares, "I carried you on eagles' wings and brought you to myself." You are not flying alone. God is your lift, your strength, your guide.

So, lead like an Eagle, with power rooted in humility, vision anchored in God's purpose, and accountability that reflects His heart. When you do, not only will you soar, but you'll help others rise and step into everything God has called them to be.

CHAPTER 5

THE UNSEEN LEADER

An Ant's Mission

IN THE EARLY YEARS OF our ministry, there was always more work than there were hands to do it. I had a vision, but vision alone doesn't answer phones, pay bills, or keep the lights on. Like many pastors, I was bi-vocational, dividing my time between my regular job and the never-ending needs of the church. The administrative load alone could have been enough to discourage even the most passionate leader.

Yet, during this overwhelming season, there was one person who embodied the spirit of the Ant: faithful, steady, and grounded. No task was too small, and no burden was too heavy for her willing hands. I remember asking one day, "Who can answer the church phones at least two days a week?"

Without hesitation, she spoke up. "I will do it, Pastor Luke."

I asked, "Who can ensure the bills are paid, prayer requests are answered, money is counted, and the bathroom supplies are ordered?"

Again, she stepped forward. "Don't worry about it, Pastor Luke, I will do it."

Her response was always the same: calm, confident, and unwavering.

"Are you sure this is not too much?" I asked, concerned that the weight of so many responsibilities might overwhelm her.

She smiled and said, "Absolutely not, sir. I can do all things through Christ who strengthens me."

She didn't lead from the pulpit or the platform, but she led through faithfulness. While others sought recognition, she sought results. While some questioned whether I saw their work, she remained steadfast, knowing that God saw it.

Her commitment reminds me of the wisdom in Proverbs 6:6-8: "Go to the ant, you sluggard; consider its ways and be wise! It has no commander, no overseer or ruler, yet it stores its provisions in summer and gathers its food at harvest."

She didn't need a title to lead. She didn't need applause to stay motivated. She worked—not for attention—but because she believed in the vision. The Ant in leadership teaches us that success is not built on moments of inspiration but on a foundation of consistent, diligent work. It's not about who gets the credit; it's about ensuring that the work gets done.

> *Their ideas may not always be flashy, but they are almost always effective.*

Because of her, the ministry had stability. Because of her, I could focus on the vision of leading the people, preparing sermons, etc. Because of her faithfulness, the ministry didn't just survive—it thrived. She was an Ant, and the kingdom of God is built by people like her. Thank you, Ms. A.

DILIGENCE IN THE SHADOWS: SPOTTING THE ANT ON YOUR TEAM

In the LEAD Model, the Ant represents diligence, dependability, and grounded wisdom. Ants aren't flashy, but they are faithful. They don't need applause to do the work; they just do it. For a pastor, discerning the Ant personality within your ministry team can be one of the greatest blessings for sustained progress and long-term fruitfulness. Here's how to recognize them and why they're essential.

They Work Without a Stage

The Ant isn't looking for recognition; they're focused on results. Often found in quiet roles like setting up chairs, balancing the books, or maintaining order behind the scenes, Ants are defined by their consistency, not their charisma. They're usually the first to arrive and the last to leave, and they complete tasks without needing to be asked twice. Ants thrive on structure, follow direction well, and stay loyal to the mission, not their ego. Titles don't motivate them; results do. They're not part of the paparazzi or groupie crowd; they serve faithfully without drama, seeking no spotlight . . . just doing the work that matters.

They Steady the Ship

When storms hit, whether internal or external, Ants remain calm. Their presence brings stability because the team knows that they have someone in the foxhole who has their back. They're not reactionary. When others are panicking, the Ant is troubleshooting and making a list.

They typically are the team member who brings peace during pressure, who values structure, and who resists chaos with quiet calm.

They Offer Practical, Grounded Solutions

Ants aren't dreamers or visionaries. They are doers. Their ideas may not always be flashy, but they are almost always effective. When faced with problems, they look for logical, resourceful answers. They are typically the ones who simplify complex issues and ask, "What's the next step we can take?" They may even say, "We are not here to write the vision, only to enforce it!"

They Steward Resources Well

Whether managing time, money, or manpower, Ants don't waste. They don't overspend, overcommit, or overpromise. Instead, they maximize what's available. Their stewardship helps prevent burnout and budget blowouts. If something is missing on the spreadsheet, budget sheet, invoice, or itemized list, they will find it. They are typically the ones who track details, stick to timelines, and always have a "Plan B."

They Carry More Than You Think

Just like real ants, they're stronger than they look. You may not notice how much they're carrying until they're gone. They carry burdens silently, working without needing praise. Ants are very hard to replace. Although they are easy to find in the real ant world, they are not so easy to find in leadership.

They are typically the team member who always says, "I've got it," and actually *does*—every single time.

WHY PASTORS NEED ANTS

In a world that often celebrates the loudest voices, pastors must learn to value the faithful hands. Ants may never ask for a microphone, but without them, the ministry doesn't move forward. They build the foundation others stand on. Their diligence in the shadows is proof of spiritual maturity and kingdom-first living.

> *Ants are the backbone of any ministry.*

Leading someone with an Ant personality requires intentional care, respect for their wiring, and clarity in communication. Ants thrive under healthy leadership that understands and honors their steady, behind-the-scenes strength.

Here's how a pastor can best lead and steward someone with an Ant personality:

1) **Provide clear structure and expectations:** Ants thrive in order. They like knowing what's expected, what the process is, and how they fit into the larger mission. Ambiguity can frustrate them or cause them to shut down.
   Do: Give clear instructions, timelines, and roles.
   Don't: Be vague or constantly change the plan without explanation.
2) **Respect their faithfulness:** Ants are faithful, and they take their work seriously, even if it's "small." A pastor can lead them well by simply acknowledging their quiet strength and consistency. They don't need the spotlight, but every now and then, a genuine "thank you" means everything. Knowing that you are pleased with their contribution is their reward.
   Do: Celebrate their reliability in private or small ways.
   Don't: Take their service for granted or assume they don't need encouragement.
3) **Don't overload them—even though you could:** Ants will carry heavy loads, and they'll do it without complaining. But that doesn't mean it's sustainable. Pastors need to pay attention to what Ants won't say. Just because they "can" doesn't mean they "should."
   Do: Check in regularly and help them prioritize.
   Don't: Just keep giving them more because they won't say no.
4) **Include them in planning:** Ants bring practical insight. They may not speak up often, but when they do, they're usually right. They're rooted in reality and logic, so involving them in the planning process can bring major clarity.

Do: Ask their opinion, especially when planning logistics or problem-solving. They are better at telling you "how" than "why."

Don't: Assume they're not thinking just because they're not talking.

5) **Give them room to work:** Ants value autonomy and trust. Once they understand the mission and the goal, they're more than capable of running with it. Micromanaging can feel like mistrust.

Do: Empower them with the freedom to execute.

Don't: Hover or second-guess their process if they're producing results.

6) **Lead with consistency:** The Ant personality often mirrors the leadership they serve under. If a pastor is erratic, indecisive, or unclear, it throws them off. They value consistent leadership just as much as they offer consistent service.

Do: Be dependable in your leadership—follow through on your word.

Don't: Be inconsistent in expectations or tone.

Ants don't just need vision; they need a steady voice. Ants are the backbone of any ministry. To bring out the best in an Ant, it's important to understand their needs, strengths, and communication style. The Ant is defined by faithfulness, diligence, and consistency, which is why I believe that they are the backbone of any team. However, they can sometimes struggle with flexibility and burnout if not properly supported. When pastors lead them well—with clarity, care, and consistency—they don't just serve; they thrive. And when they thrive, the whole ministry gets stronger.

GROWTH AREAS FOR THE ANT

While the Ant brings incredible value through diligence, consistency, and humble service, even the most faithful team members have room to grow. Recognizing these growth areas isn't about fixing weaknesses; it's about stretching strengths, developing balance, and unlocking even greater potential. As we explore these areas, we'll see how Ants can grow into even more effective, resilient, and impactful leaders.

Flexibility and Adaptability

Ants love structure, but ministry is often unpredictable. Sudden changes, unplanned needs, or visionary pivots can stress them out. They may resist or shut down when their routine is disrupted.

Help them to learn to trust the process and to trust God even when the plan shifts. Practice staying calm in chaos and see change as an opportunity to grow, not a threat to order.

Speaking Up with Confidence

Ants often defer to others and stay behind the scenes. While humble, they may withhold valuable ideas, insights, or concerns that could help the team.

Ants should step into moments where their voice matters. Convince them that their input is valuable, and they shouldn't be afraid to speak up, even if they are not the loudest in the room.

Big-Picture Thinking

Because they're so task-focused, Ants can get caught in the weeds and miss the bigger vision. They may struggle to see how their piece fits into God's greater purpose.

Encourage them to zoom out regularly. They should ask leaders to help them connect their role to the bigger mission. Vision fuels endurance.

Saying "No" or Setting Boundaries

Ants will keep taking on work until they burn out. Their loyalty is admirable, but they can overextend themselves out of a desire to serve.

Help them to see that it's not unfaithful to rest. Teach them that boundaries protect their ability to serve long-term. Saying "no" at the right time is an act of stewardship.

Navigating Emotion and Conflict

Ants tend to avoid conflict, preferring peace and predictability. This can lead to bottling up emotions or avoiding hard conversations.

Encourage them to practice addressing issues lovingly but directly. Healthy conflict can strengthen teams. Don't allow them to let their need for calm silence interfere with communication.

Embracing Risk and Innovation

Ants are grounded in practicality, which sometimes makes them risk-averse. They may hesitate when faith requires stepping into the unknown. Encourage them to balance their wisdom with boldness.

Ants are vital to any team, but just like any leadership style, they're not the whole picture. When Ants grow in adaptability, courage, and voice, they become not just dependable doers but influential leaders in their own right. By embracing growth in these areas, the Ant can enhance their leadership impact, deepen their relationships, and serve with greater balance and effectiveness.

For leaders and team members working with an Ant, understanding their unique needs is essential to helping them thrive. Take the time to get to know them and show genuine interest in their well-being. Creating a safe and secure environment helps them feel valued and appreciated. Place them in roles or groups where there is little to no conflict. Ants excel in harmonious environments and may struggle in high-pressure or confrontational settings.

AM I THE ANT?

Now that we've unpacked how to identify the Ant, it's worth asking: *Could I be the Ant?*

Many pastors quietly carry the weight of the ministry without seeking attention or applause. If you're naturally drawn to structure, systems, and getting the job done, no matter who notices, you just might be an Ant yourself. Ant pastors lead with consistency, humility, and a deep sense of responsibility, often building ministries that are solid, sustainable, and steady.

Here are a few key indicators you may be an Ant:
- You prefer **systems over spontaneity** and love a good calendar or checklist.
- You feel most useful when you're **serving quietly behind the scenes**. You say things like, "Please don't put my photo in the bulletin or the church website," or, "I would rather not have my name on the church bus."

- You tend to **take on a lot of responsibility**, often without asking for help.
- You're a **steady hand in storms**; people count on your calm presence.
- You value **faithfulness over flash**, and you'd rather be reliable than remarkable.
- You often **downplay your contributions**, even when others praise your work.
- You're intentional about how you use time, money, and resources, **a natural steward**.
- You feel uncomfortable in the spotlight but thrive when working **toward a shared goal**.

If this sounds like you, pastor, then you may be a pastor-Ant, a vital kind of leader in the kingdom. You are the foundation others build on. Your ministry may not always grab headlines, but it will stand the test of time. Embrace your Ant identity and lean into the strengths God has wired into your leadership. Just remember: even Ants need rest, vision, and support. You were never meant to carry it all alone.

CHAPTER 6

THE PEACEFUL LEADER

A Dove's Quiet Power

IN THE EARLY YEARS OF my ministry, I was full of excitement about building a strong team, one that could help carry the vision forward. I noticed a young man who faithfully attended every Sunday and mid-week service. He asked thoughtful questions about the Bible and showed a deep zeal for ministry. I was impressed by his passion for knowledge and quickly arranged a meeting with him. During our conversation, he shared that he felt a deep calling to be a minister of the gospel and his desire to serve in some capacity at our church.

Eager to support his journey and excited about the opportunity to have this young, vibrant mind as a part of our ministry team, I enrolled him in our Minister in Training (MIT) program. He was inquisitive yet quiet, confident yet reserved, a peaceful presence among his peers. After completing the program, I licensed him as a minister and assigned him to work under a seasoned leader in our youth department. He always wore a smile and never voiced a complaint, so I assumed he was content and thriving in his new role.

But a few weeks later, I noticed a pattern of frequent absences. One missed Sunday turned into two, and eventually, weeks turned into months. Concerned, I called to check in with him. That's when he quietly shared that he felt overwhelmed by the demands of the youth ministry. He hadn't spoken up because he didn't want to disappoint the team. Instead of saying anything to me or to the student pastor, he chose to step away from the church.

> *Peacemaking Doves are like spiritual shock absorbers—they don't stop conflict from happening, but they soften the impact.*

His story taught me a critical truth: peace in leadership isn't just about calm; it's about discernment. As leaders, we should be sensitive to the Dove's silent signals. A peaceful leader doesn't just listen to words; they notice the absence of them also.

LEADERSHIP TRAITS OF THE DOVE

In the LEAD Model, the Dove represents a personality type characterized by peace, compassion, empathy, and a nurturing spirit. This personality type can play a vital role in maintaining harmony within the ministry and often excels in roles that require listening, counseling, and emotional support. Let's discuss some of the traits of the Dove personality.

Peacemaking

The Dove thrives in an atmosphere of harmony and unity. When conflict arises within the ministry, this individual naturally steps in as a calming presence, seeking resolution with grace and sensitivity. Rather than fueling division or taking sides, the Dove listens attentively and helps all parties feel heard. Their goal isn't to win arguments but to restore relationships. Oftentimes, they become quiet mediators between dominant or opposing personalities, helping bring clarity and calm where tension once ruled.

Peacemaking Doves are like spiritual shock absorbers—they don't stop conflict from happening, but they soften the impact. They carry a ministry of reconciliation, and in doing so, they protect the mission, strengthen the community, and lighten the pastor's emotional load.

Compassionate and Caring

At the heart of the Dove's nature is deep empathy. They not only recognize the emotions of others but also often carry those feelings with them, whether joy or sorrow. This sensitivity makes them incredibly nurturing and approachable. When someone is hurting, the Dove offers more than words; they offer presence, encouragement, and sincere care. Their compassion is not performative or fleeting; it's a core part of who they are and how they express God's love to others.

Compassionate and caring Doves are the church's emotional first responders. They keep the body of Christ tender, connected, and spiritually responsive, and in doing so, they amplify the pastor's reach and protect the emotional health of the flock.

Loyal and Supportive

Doves are the steady hearts of the ministry. While others may come and go with changing seasons, the Dove remains faithful, often showing up when no one else does. They don't crave public recognition or leadership titles; they simply want to serve. Their loyalty is quiet but powerful, offering a kind of stability that pastors and leaders deeply rely on. In difficult seasons, they don't panic or abandon ship; instead, they dig in deeper, offering encouragement and help wherever needed.

Loyal and supportive, Doves keep the ministry team together in spirit and focused in mission. For the pastor, they provide a foundation of faithfulness that helps sustain leadership through every season.

Gentle and Soft-Spoken

A Dove leads not through authority or charisma but through a gentle spirit. Their words are measured and calm, often diffusing tension simply by their tone and demeanor. While others may speak loudly or assertively, the Dove's quiet strength creates a safe space for others to express themselves. They model how leadership doesn't always need to be bold or brash; sometimes, the most powerful influence is soft and sincere. Their presence tends to comfort and reassure, especially in emotionally charged moments.

Gentle and soft-spoken, Doves create a peaceful culture that improves communication, trust, and emotional health. Their strength lies not in volume but in consistency, kindness, and quiet wisdom, all of which strengthen the team and bring valuable emotional support to the pastor.

Doves are often the ones who approach the pastor with discernment and grace, offering insights or concerns in a respectful and uplifting way. Their tone softens hard truths, making it easier for the pastor to receive correction or feedback without feeling attacked. In short, their communication style helps build healthy, life-giving dialogue between the leader and the team.

Spiritually Sensitive

The Dove is deeply attuned to the spiritual and emotional environment around them. They often spend time in prayer and quiet reflection, which heightens their discernment. This spiritual sensitivity allows them to sense when something is off, even before it's spoken. Doves may not always speak up immediately, but their insight is often profound and Spirit-led. Pastors can trust the Dove to be a prayer warrior, an intercessor, and someone who hears from God with humility and clarity.

Spiritually sensitive, Dove leaders create a covering of prayer and discernment over the ministry. They help the team stay aligned with the Spirit and offer the pastor quiet but powerful support that can't be measured in meetings but is deeply felt in moments of breakthrough and peace.

For the pastor, having a spiritually sensitive Dove on the team is like having an early warning system and a quiet intercessor. These individuals often sense when the pastor is tired, spiritually drained, or carrying unseen pressure. And instead of confronting loudly, they pray fervently. They cover the pastor, discern spiritual warfare, and often bring a word in season—gently, humbly, and with clarity.

DISCOVERING THE DOVE: SPOTTING THE GENTLE SPIRIT IN MINISTRY

Without Doves, the church becomes a machine—functional but emotionally cold. With them, it becomes a family. Pastors, as you identify Doves in your midst, you must not overlook or underestimate them. These quiet warriors carry the spirit of peace, love, and endurance. They are, quite literally, the glue that holds the house together. Listed are a few ways to identify the Doves that serve in ministry:

1) **Observe how they respond to conflict.** The Dove reveals itself most clearly in moments of tension. When disagreements arise in ministry, whether among leaders, congregants, or staff, the Dove instinctively seeks unity. They aren't looking to win arguments or dominate conversations. Their heart is to mend what's broken and restore harmony.

    You will rarely find a Dove stirring up drama or escalating a situation. In fact, they often grow visibly uncomfortable when tempers rise or voices get loud. Their gentle demeanor is not a sign of weakness but of strength under control. The Dove carries the ministry of reconciliation, moving quietly but intentionally to bring healing where there is hurt. If you want to recognize a Dove in your leadership team, watch how they handle division. Chances are, they're trying to build a bridge while others are choosing sides.

2) **Notice their role in community and care.** The Dove often finds its place in ministries that reflect the heart of compassion. While others may be drawn to leadership roles or strategic planning, the Dove gravitates toward spaces where emotional support, presence, and peace are needed most. You'll frequently find them serving in areas like hospitality, counseling, intercession, or care teams, not for recognition but because they are wired to nurture.

Doves have a calming presence that draws people in. When someone on the team or in ministry is hurting, discouraged, or simply needs a safe place to be heard, they naturally turn to the Dove. These gentle souls offer more than sympathy; they offer Spirit-led comfort and a nonjudgmental ear. If you want to identify a Dove in your ministry, look for the one quietly caring behind the scenes, faithfully showing up where people need tenderness and truth in equal measure.

3) **Listen to how they speak.** The voice of the Dove is unmistakable, not in volume but in tone. Their words carry a gentle weight, often seasoned with grace and encouragement. While others may lean into bold declarations or sharp critiques, the Dove chooses language that soothes, uplifts, and seeks peace. In conversations, meetings, or moments of correction, they instinctively speak in a way that draws hearts together rather than pushing them apart.

Even under pressure, Doves rarely resort to harsh or negative speech. Their desire for unity is evident in how they phrase even difficult truths with compassion and humility. You may notice that they're the ones calming heated discussions, offering affirming words, or reminding others of the bigger picture. If you're listening closely, the Dove's voice will sound a lot like the fruit of the Spirit—gentle, kind, and full of love.

EMPOWERING THE DOVE: STRENGTHENING THE QUIET LEADER

To empower a Dove in ministry, a pastor must first recognize the quiet strength they carry. Doves often serve behind the scenes, not seeking the spotlight but faithfully nurturing the flock with compassion, prayer, and emotional support. They may not demand a platform, but they flourish when their contributions are acknowledged and valued, especially by the pastor. A wise pastor empowers the Dove by creating safe spaces where their gentleness is not mistaken for weakness, and their peacemaking gifts are seen as vital to the health of the church body.

Pastors can also empower Doves by inviting them into roles that align with their strengths: care ministries, prayer teams, counseling support, or mentoring others through seasons of brokenness. Give them room to lead in ways that feel authentic to their nature. Encourage them to share their voice in meetings or decision-making settings where emotional intelligence and spiritual sensitivity are needed. Most importantly, speak life into their identity. Let them know that their softness is not a liability; it is a reflection of Christ's heart. When a Dove feels seen, supported, and spiritually covered, they soar.

AREAS OF GROWTH: DEVELOPING THE DOVE'S LEADERSHIP CAPACITY

While the Dove brings a deep well of gentleness, empathy, and peacemaking into ministry, these strengths can also present areas for intentional growth. During my years of ministry, one common challenge for the Dove that I have noticed is the tendency to avoid conflict altogether. Their desire for unity can sometimes lead them to suppress truth or withdraw from necessary confrontation. A pastor can lovingly guide a Dove to see that biblical peace is not the absence of tension but the presence of morality. Helping them build confidence in speaking truth, in love, equips them to grow into more balanced and courageous leaders.

> *Peacemaking is active, not passive.*

Another area of development is in confident decision-making and assertiveness. Because Doves are highly relational, they may struggle with making firm choices that might disappoint others or stir disapproval. They can default to people-pleasing or hesitate when bold action is needed. Pastors can encourage Doves to trust the Holy Spirit's guidance and affirm that saying "no" can be just as godly as saying "yes." Teaching them how to set healthy boundaries and reminding them that leadership sometimes involves tension will help them develop both spiritual maturity and emotional resilience.

Lastly, Doves may need support in recognizing their own leadership value. Their quieter demeanor can make them feel overshadowed in rooms filled with other personality traits. But when nurtured and affirmed, Doves bring balance, heart, and healing to any ministry team. Pastors can empower Doves to believe that their voice matters, and when they find the courage to use it, the entire body of Christ is strengthened.

"Blessed are the peacemakers, for they will be called children of God" (Matthew 5:9) affirms the Dove's core identity, but it also carries a quiet challenge: peacemaking is active, not passive. True peacemakers are willing to step into difficult spaces, speak truth in love, and help others walk in reconciliation. Growth for the Dove often begins when they understand that their voice, though gentle, is powerful when led by the Spirit.

"For God has not given us a spirit of fear, but of power and of love and of a sound mind" (2 Timothy 1:7, NKJV) is especially helpful for the Dove who may struggle with fear of conflict, rejection, or stepping forward. God has equipped them with all they need, not just to comfort others but to lead with clarity, conviction, and courage.

WHEN THE DOVE LEADS: A SPIRITUAL MIRROR FOR GENTLE SHEPHERDS

Not every pastor leads with a roar or soars with vision from the heights. Some lead with a quiet strength, a calming presence, and a deep, Spirit-led compassion. If you've ever felt like the "gentle one" in the room, you might be wondering, Am I the Dove?

This question is not about whether you're soft-spoken or introverted. It's about the spiritual posture that you bring to leadership. The Dove is a symbol of peace, grace, and reconciliation. In Scripture, the dove represents the Holy Spirit descending with gentleness (Matthew 3:16) and the peace Noah saw after the storm (Genesis 8:11). Doves in ministry carry that same calming presence—they seek healing over conflict, harmony over hierarchy, and compassion over competition.

Pastor, if you are a Dove at heart, you may notice the following:

- **You prioritize unity and emotional wellness** over aggressive forward motion.
- **You are often the one others come to** when they're hurting, confused, or seeking comfort.
- **You're more inclined to mediate than to mandate**, often diffusing tension with quiet words and a listening ear.
- **You may struggle with confrontation or decision-making**, especially when it risks upsetting someone.

While these qualities can sometimes feel like a disadvantage in high-energy leadership spaces, they are actually essential to a healthy, Spirit-led ministry team.

QUESTIONS FOR PASTORAL REFLECTION

Use these questions to explore whether you lead like a Dove:

- Do I feel more fulfilled in roles that involve caring, praying, or nurturing?
- Do I naturally avoid conflict, even when something needs to be addressed?

- Have I felt overshadowed or underestimated because I lead with gentleness?
- Do people seek me out for emotional support or spiritual counsel?
- Am I more focused on maintaining peace than "winning" or controlling outcomes?

Answering "yes" to many of these may reveal Dove-like tendencies within your leadership style. Take a few moments to reflect on the following questions, either in prayer or in your journal:

- In what situations do I tend to stay silent, even when I sense God calling me to speak?
- Am I avoiding necessary conflict out of fear, or am I pursuing true peace?
- What would it look like for me to lead from a place of quiet strength instead of shrinking back?
- How can I grow in setting boundaries while still carrying the heart of compassion?

If your leadership style is predominantly that of a Dove, you are not less of a leader; you are a different kind of leader. Your ministry may not always be loud, but it is deeply felt. In a world of noise, your quiet obedience, consistent compassion, and Spirit-led discernment are profoundly powerful. The body of Christ needs your presence, your prayer life, and your peacekeeping heart.

You are not a passive leader; you are a peacemaking one. And that's a holy calling.

CHAPTER 7

FOUR PERSONALITIES, ONE VISION

Unlocking the Synergy of the LEAD Model Team

IN THE BODY OF ANY ministry, unity doesn't always mean uniformity. God, in His infinite wisdom, created us uniquely—each with different strengths, perspectives, and approaches. The LEAD Model reveals four distinct leadership personalities: Lion, Eagle, Ant, and Dove, each valuable in ministry, each essential for healthy leadership teams. But can these vastly different personality types work together without conflict? And how can an executive leader lead them in harmony?

THE POWER OF BALANCE

When a Lion roars alone, it may inspire fear or command respect, but when joined by the soaring perspective of the Eagle, the diligence of the Ant, and the compassion of the Dove, something powerful happens—balance.

Each personality compensates for the weaknesses of the other, forming a leadership team that is whole, wise, and effective. This is the beauty of God's design: just as the human body has many parts with different functions yet operates as one (Romans 12:4), so ministry teams should operate in unity and diversity. As Paul reminds us in 1 Corinthians 12, the church is one body made up of many members, each with a unique function, and every member of the body is necessary and valuable. None can say to the other, "I have no need of you." The eye cannot say to the hand, "I don't need you!" (v. 21, NKJV), nor can the head dismiss the foot. When these four personalities work in harmony, they don't just reflect good leadership; they reflect Christ Himself, leading His church through a unified, Spirit-filled team.

In the same way, the Lion is not greater than the Dove, nor is the Eagle more important than the Ant. Each plays a vital role, and each must be honored.

THE LEADERSHIP MOSAIC: DIFFERENT BY DESIGN BUT STRONGER TOGETHER

Leadership isn't one-size-fits-all, but when different styles and personalities are brought together in harmony, they form a priceless mosaic—uniquely diverse yet beautifully unified. The LEAD Model helps us see how diverse leadership styles can come together to form a powerful, cohesive team.

- **The Lion (L—Leads with Courage):** Leads with boldness and clarity. The Lion is the initiator and visionary, unafraid to move forward even when others hesitate.
- **The Eagle (E—Envisions with Insight):** Brings strategy and foresight. The Eagle sees the big picture and steers the team toward wise, long-term decisions.

- **The Ant (A—Acts with Diligence):** Serves through faithful, consistent work. The Ant manages the essential behind-the-scenes tasks that keep everything running smoothly.
- **The Dove (D—Delivers Peace and Care):** Offers unity and emotional intelligence. The Dove nurtures relationships, protects the heart of the people, and maintains peace within the team.

Like threads in a beautiful tapestry, the Lion, Eagle, Ant, and Dove each bring their unique colors and textures. Woven together, they create a unified masterpiece of leadership, strength, and dexterity.

Let's imagine what happens when the Lion, Eagle, Ant, and Dove operate in sync within the ministry.

The Lion steps forward with courage and conviction, setting a bold goal for the church's outreach ministry. With strength and clarity, the Lion declares a vision that galvanizes the ministry, a vision that calls the people to rise and reach their community in new and daring ways.

The Eagle, ever watchful and spiritually discerning, then takes that vision and charts the course. With keen foresight and prophetic sensitivity, the Eagle anticipates obstacles, aligns the mission with divine timing, and ensures that the vision remains grounded in God's Word and in line with the mission of the church.

Meanwhile, the Ant quietly begins organizing. With diligence and focus, the Ant mobilizes volunteers, creates systems, manages resources, and ensures the details are executed with excellence. The Ant is focused not on flashy displays but on steady, faithful work that makes the vision attainable.

Then comes the Dove, whose gentle spirit ministers to the hearts of the team. The Dove ensures that the emotional and spiritual well-being of everyone is cared for. Through encouragement, prayer, and a listening ear, the Dove creates a safe and nurturing atmosphere that binds the team together in unity and love, checking on every team member and making sure that everyone is okay mentally, physically, and spiritually.

When the body works together in love and mutual respect, empowered by the Spirit, it reflects the fullness of Christ's leadership. That's the beauty of the LEAD Model: it reminds us that the church flourishes not when one type of leader dominates but when all are embraced and empowered to serve in their God-given strength.

Years ago, I witnessed this harmony firsthand while leading a countywide outreach event during the COVID-19 pandemic. The idea began with a Lion on our leadership team who felt stirred by God to take bold action and address the food insecurity needs of those within our county, a large-scale evangelistic effort that would reach neighborhoods often overlooked by the church. The vision was compelling, but it was the Eagle who took that vision and mapped it out. With spiritual discernment and strategic planning, the Eagle developed a plan that not only provided food to those in need but also opened the door for our church to disciple new believers.

> *Shepherding each leadership type requires spiritual discernment, relational wisdom, and strategic management.*

The Ants on the team were invaluable. While others spoke on stages and cast vision, it was the Ants who arrived early, set up chairs, managed registration, coordinated food pickups, and ensured every single element of the event ran smoothly. They didn't seek applause; they simply got the job done.

And then, in the quiet places, the Doves were at work. They prayed with people as they came through the lines to pick up food. They comforted those who were unsure or overwhelmed. They ministered behind the scenes to our volunteers, reminding each person that what they were doing mattered. When tensions rose or someone felt overlooked, it was the Dove who brought peace and restored unity.

The event was a success, not just because people came to Christ but because every leader played their part. The Lion, Eagle, Ant, and Dove operated in alignment, like a symphony, each instrument distinct yet beautifully coordinated. As a pastor, this was one of my proudest moments in ministry, being a part of the body that reached the people. When we recognize and empower each part of the LEAD team, we don't just build ministries; we build the kingdom.

A wise pastor doesn't treat every leader the same. Shepherding each leadership type requires spiritual discernment, relational wisdom, and strategic management.

LION

Profile: Bold but Beware

Strengths:
- Courageous and decisive
- Visionary initiator
- Inspires movement and momentum

Dysfunctional Lion: When dysfunctional, the Lion exhibits dominance without empathy and controlling or aggressive behavior that stifles collaboration.

Example

In a church planning meeting, Pastor John (a Lion-type leader) stormed in with a new ministry initiative. Without waiting for input, he declared the direction, assigned roles, and expected immediate execution. The Dove on his team, Sister West, felt unseen and emotionally drained. Brother Pugh (an Eagle-type leader) tried to interject with a long-term strategy, but Pastor Noel (the Ant-type leader) shut it down with, "We don't have time for all that."

What Happened?

- The Dove withdrew emotionally, feeling undervalued.
- The Eagle disengaged, sensing that his wisdom wasn't welcome.
- The Ant complied but grew quietly resentful due to the unrealistic timeline.

The Outcome

The project launched quickly but collapsed due to a lack of planning, poor morale, and relational tension.

What Could Have Been Done Differently?

The Lion's aggressive pursuit of goals may create a fast-paced environment but one that sacrifices the steady foundation the Ant provides and the wise direction the Eagle offers, ultimately compromising the health and sustainability of the mission. Had the Lion paused to consult the Eagle for strategic planning, listened to the Dove's concerns, and invited the Ant to shape the execution plan, the team would have been unified and the launch sustainable. The Lion's vision, guided by collaboration, would have roared with lasting impact.

EAGLE

Profile: Wise but Withdrawing

Strengths:
- Strategic and forward-thinking
- Sees the big picture
- Offers wisdom and long-term clarity

Dysfunctional Eagle: When dysfunctional, the Eagle becomes aloof, overly critical, and paralyzed by perfectionism.

Example

Deacon Maya (an Eagle-type) was asked to help develop the church's outreach plan. Instead of acting, she spent weeks mapping data, analyzing trends, and creating elaborate presentations.

The Ant grew frustrated waiting for direction, and the Lion began pushing ahead without her input.

What Happened?
- The Lion launched without Maya, missing key strategies.
- The Ant, caught in the middle, had to constantly adapt.
- The Dove felt the tension and began trying to mediate.

The Outcome
The outreach was ineffective because it lacked structure and heart. Maya felt bitter that her insight wasn't used, even though she hadn't communicated clearly.

What Could Have Been Done Differently?
Maya could have shared a concise plan early and then iterated along the way. Partnering with the Ant for execution and inviting the Dove to shape relational tone would've brought her vision to life in a timely, impactful way.

ANT

Profile: Faithful but Frustrated

Strengths:
- Diligent and consistent
- Keeps systems running
- Humble and task-oriented

Dysfunctional Ant: When unhealthy, the Ant becomes overwhelmed, resentful, and resistant to change.

Example

Brother Rick (an Ant-type) had been running the media ministry faithfully for five years. When the Eagle suggested automating a few systems to improve efficiency, Rick took it personally. He resisted every proposal, claiming, "It's always worked this way."

What Happened?

- The Eagle became frustrated with the lack of progress.
- The Lion considered replacing Rick to "just get it done."
- The Dove felt caught between both sides, fearing division.

The Outcome

The ministry stagnated. Rick burned out but wouldn't ask for help. Others didn't feel free to step in.

What Could Have Been Done Differently?

If Rick had seen change as a form of stewardship rather than criticism, he could have worked with the Eagle to implement improvements gradually. With affirmation from the Dove and clarity from the Lion, he could have grown instead of burning out.

DOVE

Profile: Peaceful but Passive

Strengths:
- Nurturing and empathetic
- Promotes harmony and care
- Excellent at maintaining team unity

Dysfunctional Dove: The Dove, when dysfunctional, avoids conflict, enables dysfunction, and values peace over progress.

Example

Sister Naomi (a Dove-type) noticed growing tension between the Ant and the Lion over Sunday service logistics. Rather than address it, she smoothed things over with kind words and a smile. She even redid some tasks herself just to avoid confrontation.

What Happened?

- The Ant became more resentful, seeing Naomi as taking sides.
- The Lion interpreted Naomi's silence as agreement and pressed harder.
- The Eagle felt the whole system was off but couldn't get a clear answer from anyone.

The Outcome

Tensions erupted later in a staff meeting. Misunderstandings had grown, and people felt emotionally abandoned or unheard.

What Could Have Been Done Differently?

If Naomi had gently but firmly addressed the conflict early, perhaps by mediating a conversation between the Lion and the Ant, issues could have been resolved with clarity and grace. Her gift of peace would have protected the team, not prolonged the pain.

BEYOND PERSONALITIES: DEVELOPING TEAMS THAT THINK AND WIN TOGETHER

The executive leader's leadership goes beyond managing individuals; it is about shaping a culture where each person feels seen, valued, and strategically aligned. In a healthy team culture, Lions, Eagles, Ants, and Doves don't just coexist; they collaborate. For this to happen, the pastor must intentionally steward the emotional and spiritual climate of the team. Let's explore how this can be accomplished.

Teach Appreciation

One of the most powerful ways that a pastor can build unity is by publicly acknowledging the value of each leadership type. When you celebrate the Lion's courage, the Eagle's insight, the Ant's diligence, and the Dove's compassion from the pulpit or in team meetings, you reinforce that every gift matters. This isn't flattery; it's biblical. Romans 12:10 says, "Honor one another above yourselves." A culture of appreciation lifts morale, affirms identity, and helps each personality understand their unique role in the kingdom. Regular encouragement also dismantles competition and replaces it with celebration.

Facilitate Communication

Each type in the LEAD Model has its own "language." Lions speak in action and urgency, Eagles in vision and analysis, Ants in systems and tasks, and Doves in feelings and relationships. Without intentional communication, their differences can create distance instead of connection. A wise pastor creates structured opportunities for dialogue, staff meetings, feedback sessions, and team-building moments that encourage mutual respect and active listening. James 1:19 reminds us to be "quick to listen, slow to speak, and slow to become angry." When the pastor models this posture, communication becomes a bridge rather than a battleground.

Model Humility

The pastor sets the tone for honor in the house. By openly recognizing the contributions of each type and not exalting one over another, the leader reinforces the truth of 1 Corinthians 12:21: "The eye cannot say to the hand, 'I don't need you!'" When pastors model humility, they permit others to do the same. This dismantles pride and hierarchy and builds a team identity where every part is necessary. Let the team see you defer, delegate, and depend on others. When humility is visible at the top, unity flows through the body.

Deal with Conflict with Compassion and Clarity

Conflict is inevitable, but how it's handled determines whether a team is strengthened or split. A collaborative culture doesn't avoid conflict; it processes it with maturity. Pastors must lead the way by applying the principles of Matthew 18:15-17: private correction first, then inclusive dialogue, if necessary, all wrapped in love. Lions may rush to judgment, Doves may retreat, Ants may suppress it, and Eagles may over-analyze it, but biblical confrontation teaches every personality to handle tension with grace. A team that knows how to resolve issues in love is a team built to last.

LEADING IN HARMONY: THE STRENGTH OF UNIFIED LEADERSHIP

Ministry leadership was never meant to be a solo act; it's a divine collaboration. Just as a skilled conductor leads an orchestra, the pastor's role is to recognize, align, and release the unique sounds of each leadership type. The Lion brings bold rhythm through strength and authority. The Eagle adds depth and direction with visionary insight. The Ant provides a steady tempo with diligence and order. The Dove infuses harmony through compassion and unity.

> *To lead others well, we must be able to step into their world, see through their lens, and communicate in ways that resonate with their reality.*

When these God-given personalities operate in sync, under the lordship of Christ and the intentional leadership of a wise pastor or executive leader, the result is more than productivity—it's power with purpose. This is not just leadership; it is kingdom orchestration. The church becomes a living symphony, where every leader plays their part in building something that reflects heaven on earth.

Pastors must shift from being merely vision-casters to culture-shapers. They must be conductors of collaborative leadership. When they empower the Lion to roar, the Eagle to soar, the Ant to labor, and the Dove to heal, they multiply impact and create a ministry model that is both sustainable and supernatural.

This is the strength of unity. This is the LEAD Model in action. And this is how churches and other faith-based organizations thrive, not through one voice alone but through a chorus of anointed leaders playing in harmony for the glory of God.

CONCLUSION

While our leadership styles may shift depending on circumstances, most of us have a dominant type that surfaces when we are in our most natural and grace-filled environment. Though we may flex across various traits, bold like the Lion in one moment and compassionate like the Dove in another, there is usually one primary style that reflects how we instinctively lead, serve, and respond. This is the core of who we are when we're operating from a place of authenticity and spiritual alignment.

As leaders, this fluidity is not a weakness; it's a strength. To lead others well, we must be able to step into their world, see through their lens, and communicate in ways that resonate with their reality. This kind of leadership is not only practical; it's biblical. Jesus exemplified this perfectly. When speaking to fishermen, He used the language of casting nets and the sea (Matthew 4:19). When ministering to farmers, He taught using parables about seeds and soil (Luke 8:5-15). When addressing the rich or those tied to wealth, He spoke about treasure, stewardship, and the heart's allegiance (Matthew 19:21-24).

This model reminds us that effective leadership is not about demanding people rise to our level; it's about meeting them where they are, just as Christ did. Paul echoed this principle in 1 Corinthians 9:22 when he said, "I have become all things to all people so that by all possible means I might save some." Wise leaders know their dominant style but lead with the flexibility and humility to connect, guide, and empower others on their terms.

Take a moment to reflect on your leadership journey:

- When you are at your best—calm, confident, and Spirit-led—which leadership type shows up most naturally?
- Do you find yourself taking bold initiative like the Lion, casting vision like the Eagle, managing details and logistics like the Ant, or creating emotional and spiritual safety like the Dove?
- How does your leadership style shape the way you communicate, solve problems, or support others?
- In what ways can you better step into the world of those you lead, like Jesus did, to guide them with clarity and compassion?

Ask the Holy Spirit to reveal your core leadership wiring and how He wants to develop it. Remember, self-awareness is the starting point for spiritual maturity and effective leadership.

As you close this book, my prayer is that you leave not merely informed but deeply inspired, awakened to the intentional, God-breathed design behind every leadership style, including your own. You were created with purpose, wired with strengths, and placed in a position not by accident but by divine appointment.

The LEAD Model is more than a personality framework; it is a kingdom strategy. One that empowers pastors and leaders to build trust, minimize conflict, and unlock the full potential of every team member. It's about more than getting along; it's about advancing the gospel with unity, clarity, and strength.

When you lead with wisdom and grace, when you honor the Lion's boldness, the Eagle's vision, the Ant's diligence, and the Dove's peace, you cultivate a culture where every gift is celebrated, every voice is heard, and every calling is fulfilled. This is not just good leadership; this is kingdom leadership.

Self-awareness and others-awareness are not optional; they are essential. They are the bedrock of transformational ministry and lasting impact.

So now, lead with boldness. Lead with humility. Lead with the unwavering confidence that God has already equipped you for this calling. And as you do, may your leadership reflect the heart of the King and bring glory to His name.

Go lead—and lead well!!

GROUP DISCUSSION QUESTIONS

Recognizing and Respecting Strengths

Group Discussion Questions **139**

IN A SMALL GROUP SETTING, invite each person to answer:
- Which LEAD personality do you most identify with and why?
- Share a time when you felt most "in your zone" in ministry or leadership. What were you doing, and how did it reflect your core personality?
- How have others' strengths (Lion, Eagle, Ant, or Dove) helped you succeed or grow as a leader?
- What might be one way you can better support someone with a different leadership style than your own?

Encourage honest, respectful dialogue. The goal is not comparison but connection, to see how the body fits together (1 Corinthians 12:18).

LEADERSHIP ACTIVITY

OBJCTIVE: **TO CREATE AWARENESS AND** appreciation of diverse leadership styles.

Materials: Four labeled sections on the floor or wall: Lion, Eagle, Ant, Dove.

INSTRUCTIONS

1) Ask each team member to stand near the section that best represents their dominant leadership type.
2) Give each group five to seven minutes to list:
   - What they naturally bring to the team
   - What kind of leadership or communication style helps them thrive
   - What stresses them or causes them to withdraw
3) Then, rotate—have one representative from each group visit another group to hear their insights.
4) Close the activity by asking:

- What did you learn about others that surprised or helped you?
- How can this understanding help us collaborate more effectively as a team?
- What will you do differently to better support someone with a different leadership style?

Wrap-up Thought: Remind everyone that no one person embodies the full image of leadership, but together, we reflect the fullness of Christ's body: diverse, gifted, and united (Ephesians 4:16).

www.ingramcontent.com/pod-product-compliance
Lightning Source LLC
Chambersburg PA
CBHW070546090426
42735CB00013B/3080